MY SPECIAL PLACE

poetry today

My Special Place

Edited by
Kelly Olsen

First published in Great Britain in 1998 by Poetry Today, an imprint of
Penhaligon Page Ltd, 12 Godric Square, Maxwell Road, Peterborough. PE2 7JJ

A Catalogue record for this book is available from the British Library.

ISBN 1 86226 084 2

Typesetting and layout, Penhaligon Page Ltd, England.
Printed and bound by Forward Press Ltd, England

Foreword

My Special Place is a compilation of poetry, featuring some of our finest poets. The book gives an insight into the essence of modern living and deals with the reality of life today. We think we have created an anthology with a universal appeal.

There are many technical aspects to the writing of poetry and *My Special Place* contains free verse and examples of more structured work from a wealth of talented poets. To choose winners from the wide range of styles and forms is a most difficult task, albeit a pleasurable one. I have tried to choose a variety, to represent the poetry of today so the winners are:

J Moore	The Sea Inside
R Davies	Temporary Disarmament
C Gibbs	Talents
B Symonds	A Hay Meadow Remembered
D Griffiths	Midnight On The Promenade

My congratulations and thanks go to them and to all of you who have contributed to *My Special Place,* and I trust you will enjoy it as much as I have.

Contents

The Sea Inside

Jane Moore

As the sun drops in the sky
I watch the waves go rolling by.
They rage and crash, white horses high
But hitting sand, they fade and die.

Tide has turned, the wind speaks soft
And gulls scream insults from aloft.
Their vacant calls sound in my ears
Like lonely children close to tears.

I sit on sand, my bare feet buried
And wonder why the tide's so hurried?
Why does the sea repeat its bouts
Of turning in and turning out?
Tomorrow's work is just the same.
Why bother with this tiresome game?

No answer does the sea
Offer up to me.
It just keeps lapping on the shore
With the mystery of unspoken law.

A ruined castle can I spy
Its tattered flag still sitting high.
The unrelenting water takes
Its substance and now all its shape.
Now what was once a fine fortress
Is sand again, a flattened mess.
Some child would weep to see it so.
The waves keep washing to and fro.

I close my eyes and hear the beat.
I feel the water on my feet.
It's time to leave, I make my tracks

But now they've gone as I look back.
The beach is smooth as small waves play.
I shall return another day,
But until then I can decide
To feel the sea I hold inside.

Temporary Disarmament

Rachel Davies

Turn on the floodlights,
open the floodgates
and we'll flow over this piece of land.

Give me magic, for one hour twenty,
tries and kicks and points aplenty.
All fifteen of you take my hand.

If my home, my city, my place of birth,
is to welcome the world to this hallowed turf,
then our offerings should be truly grand.
Replace with new, what already stands.
Arms of war
and walls of sound.
Arms of warmth.
My televised playground.

So many memories and fulfilled dreams,
are wrapped around these concrete beams.
An arena where men became dragons for a day,
for the time being, has been taken away.
Still together in union,
though situations have changed.
My weapon of intimidation and I
are temporarily estranged.

I wonder now where your seats are,
and the terrace leaning bars.
I am sure that the well kept blades,
aren't being allowed to fade.
I don't see you any more!
I can only see the clouds.
Westgate misses your shadow,
and I miss creating your crowds.

Legends have graced this broken grass.
Idols of the present and icons of the past.
My eyes may be glazed with a shade of rose,
but everyone's memories are tinted I suppose.

I shared you with thousands.
I shared you with millions.
But you only belonged to me.

Of the past I am possessive,
but the future seems impressive.
I guess we'll just have to wait and see.

A Touch Of The Sun

Marie Brown

Once more I see the snowdrops bloom
Such a lovely sight
Brightening up old winters gloom
As they shed forth their light
Delicate, dainty so pretty and sweet
Dipping heads gracefully around my feet.

Primrose glow in wintry morn
Bright'ning, light'ning fog and storm
Cheery heads are held up high
For glimpse of sun in yonder sky.

Crocus cloaked in gold and blue
Perfect colours, rich and true
Shimmering, shining, proudly stand
Close together, hand in hand.

The daffodils will soon burst forth
Facing east, west, south and north
Not fussy where they group and stand
If soil is heavy clay, or sand
Ev'ry darkened corner they lift
With golden splashes as they drift.

The flow'ring plum has branches bare
But starry flowers everywhere
Peculiar sight, one not to miss
The leaves unfurl with suns first kiss.

The leaves improve as on time goes
With shades of purple, ruby, rose
Wind blows them back and forth to show
All shades and tints, springtime aglow.

Hedge buds pop on toasty beech
As upwards for the sunbeams reach
Check it out, when all is said and done
Everything benefits from a 'touch of the sun'.

When Jack Frost has done his worst
Still the trees and hedgerows burst
They never halt the ceaseless round
Of new life, forced up from the ground.

Chamberlain Square, Birmingham

E M Spencer

So much has changed!
Everywhere is stark with concrete,
The old red brick has gone,
Even the street itself!
But the fountain splashes still,
The clock tower stands aloft,
A monument to civic pride,
Marking the hours.
I hear it chime,
I chose my eyes,
The memories flood back
Of student days so long ago,
Of times alight with hope and promise
When the future was ours
And we would change the world.
I stand here, remembering
The plans and dreams,
The good times and the bad,
And give thanks for the joys that I have known.

Exile

Eammon Buckley

Asleep among the dust bins
I heard a seabird cry
'Wake up you workless vagabond
It's emigrate or die'.
The bugs rule all the bed clothes
TB stalks through the room
Set sail for 'Pagan England'
Or stay to meet your doom'.

Awake among the dust bins
I heard that seagulls cry
I knew I must leave Dublin
A tear came to my eye
I sailed the sea of misery
My heart filled with despair
When behold! in Pagan England'
A kinder God found there!

Time The Enemy?

Muriel Murphy

My watch's slow relentless tick
Records the passing of my days.
In spring the flowers I could pick
Were like the rainbow's myriad rays,
But now, late autumn, all I find
Are muted tones of golds and greys,
And my watch's slow relentless tick
Seems speeded up from earlier days.

Cold winter is in wait out there.
Already I can see its trace
In sodden leaves and branches bare
And plants adorned with hoary lace.
But, underneath frost's icy layer
The constant snowdrop waits in grace
Until the time when she can dare
To show her ever welcome face.

She proves that hope will never die.
It just takes time off from the dance
To rest its wings so it can fly
To realms it wishes to enhance.
So! My watch's slow relentless tick,
That races as the years go by,
Will speak of pleasures still to pick
And never say 'the end is nigh.'

A Place I Was Happy

L Irving

I was closed in but could see nature all around
The sun so warm, a lilac tree, my lawn, the sky
I was outside, inside in winter, still the sun felt warm
Never hidden from east to west,
By night the moon reflected through the glass
A cat walked stealthily on the roof
Looking down at a world beyond its reach!
By day she would enter, sleep peacefully,
The birds outside could be seen but they were safe.
I ate in there, read by day or night
My peaceful haven was heaven!
Then my world turned upside-down!
I lost my job, my house was sold I needed cash . . .
The frames of glass, the roof, became someone else's heaven!
But I will never forget my conservatory!

Peter

Joan M Buckley-Trott

Peter, the rock, your name implies,
This you were given before the knowledge fell,
That you with all your sweetness never could aspire,
To do as others do, without much effort spent,
Somehow I feel that name you must have held,
Before you came to bind our family close,
Through tears, despair, but always endless hope.
You are the rock on which our life revolves.
God grant that we can give you happiness,
The ultimate reward.

Untitled

Wilma Fox

Shadow of a Spirit horse.
I live on the hoof at the top of the hill,
And race through the night when it's dark and still,
The moon and the stars are my guiding light,
I am bright and shiny and dazzling white,

My name is like silk all long and smooth,
Clipperty clop is the sound of my hooves,
My heart beats faster as I run out of breath
My nostrils on fire I am covered in sweat,

I can smell the fear as the riders close in,
I try to out run them again and again,
The herd is sleeping I must let them know,
Down to the gully the riders will go,

I gallop so fast to the brow of the hill,
Their on my tail and chasing me still,
I neigh and I whinny and raise the alarm,
The herd if rises and stampedes from harm

Here comes the riders it's a night of worry,
I know it's my duty to go down to the gully,
Trapped and surrounded my blood races with fear,
I have lost my freedom captivities here,

I feel something tight wrap round my neck,
Up comes the shout bring him down to the deck,
I rise with my hooves and show them my pride,
A gunshot rings out next second I am dead,

My spirit lives on at the top of the hill,
If you watch closely you can see me still,
I am the one who rides through the night,
And my dazzling coat is your guiding light.

Blue Heaven

Prudence Bates

I shall dive to the depths
Of that cool crisp shirt
A Mediterranean blue.

Tranquil, still and deep
No promises to keep
Into your armpit I'll crawl and sleep
My haven is you.

I shall dive to the depths
Of that cool crisp shirt
A Mediterranean blue.

Tranquil, still and deep
Far from prying eyes which peep;
On the firm raft of your chest I'll weep
My haven is you.

Scotland June 1994

Joan W Needham

Scotland your beauty entered my soul,
Your mysteries my heart away stole,
Your beauty beyond compare,
Oh! what delights I do share.

You have no idea of your mysterious
charm,
As you cast your spell and give me
calm,
Glencoe the majesty enfolded with the
past,
The mountains, the glens holding their
secret fast.

The loch's your water so still and
so calm,
Gathering the rain away from harm,
Your mountains surrounded each.
Loch and glen,
Keeping their history since I don't
know when.

The snow on the peaks, lost in the
sky,
As upwards our eyes travel so high,
As onwards and onwards God's beauties
unfold.
The delights to our eye, a joy to behold.

The Would Be Artist

Marcia Sayers

If I could paint I'd go!
I'd take my water-colours and I'd go.
I'd go to Royal Troon
and there I'd set my easel up.
With languorous strokes of brush
I'd paint the hills, the beach and sea.
I'd revel in the heather tones,
all the lovely landscape tints,
the water's inky indigo,
the blue black distant lowland hills
softly contoured by the lilac sky -
a coolly arctic northern sky
above the ice cold seas -
seas edged with rocks
where rising inlands lie
emerging as prone effigies in stone,
where one,
for all the world a giant Viking resting on the shore,
evokes such imagery from long before
it's still yet named The Sleeping Warrior.
And with my artist's eye
I'd try to catch the glint of sun glancing off the craggy waves.
I'd relish the quick silveryness of all the changing lights.
And I would mark the stretch
of smoothly damp pink granite beach
that curves around the bay,
as rimmed in creamy pale brown sand,
footprintless, uncluttered, dry,
where time and tide have left it high.
But then, I cannot paint.
I'm not an artist, I!

Without Daylight

Dan Phillips

Empty hearted wings beat towards the glowing light,
starved of the environment, that is smothered by the darkest night,
becoming bitter and twisted without a care
aching antennae twitching to the intense glare.
Kaleidoscope eyes rotate their fight,

anchored strings pull upon their might,
restless panic attacks their plight.
Tired eyes fade through a stare . . .
empty hearted wings beat.

A memory drowning in flight,
a harbour slowly drifting out of sight,
captured inside an open liar . . . where minds not dare
speak of the alter of moths prayer . . .
a silent breathe clasps their tired lungs tight,
empty hearted wings beat.

The Field Hey Ho!

Patricia Margaret Holden

We ran barefoot across the field,
Chasing the shadows of the clouds.
The early day drank the sun
And we were wild things filled with joy, joy, joy.
Hey Ho!
Flinging our arms skywards; calling one to all,
Our voices spiralling out of reach.
Kathleen, Richard, Jean and I:
Innocents dancing on the green, green, green.
Hey Ho!
With toes scrunching in the cool, wet grass,
We were young and happy then.
All in the morning warming
With me, the girls, the boy, boy, boy.
Hey Ho!
They're somewhere else now, maybe gone forever;
Yet still I see each smiling face
And we all dance together, in that special field
Inside my head - I dream, dream, dream.
Hey Ho!

The Willow Tree

Sheila Eveson Corbett

The willow weeps and mourns with me, here beside the lake,
Shedding all her tears of sorrow deep enough to drown
The sad and painful memory of a thousand yesterdays,
Sinking down to hidden depths of long ago and far away.

Time cannot hear the battle-scars where swords of words have torn
the mind,
Turned life into a lingering death, and left the soul in rivers of
blood;
Only the spirit finds the thread that gently stitches every wound,
And leads the way into the light from the dark passage of time.

Fresh winds sweep through the bulrushes and bend them into
arabesques,
Singing down their slender reeds in baritone and bass;
Tuned like strings of violins to play cadenzas that transcend
Endless years of misery with overtures of hope.

Two white doves fly high above a lakeside carpeted in flowers,
They beat their wings against the clouds, conducting choral
symphonies
That saturate the sky with such a rich cacophony of sound
That all the earth is filled with music . . . and the willow
weeps no more.

Captain's Log Storm At Sea

Susan Burton

Tranquil moments spent at sea,
this is the place to be.
Islands appearing from the hue,
sitting in what seems like heavens pew.
Blue horizons for us to view.

Gentle heaving of the swell lets us know
all is well at least until Neptune has his way,
which may happen any day!
Nothing is sure, nothing is safe,
the bleakest hour can come like a race.
Winning first place.

Rageing like a forest fire that no one can quell,
is this the inferno of hell?
The pounding waves cannot put out the fire that burns
within the sea,
maybe this is not for me!

At last the thirst is quenched, this rage subsides like
a child who cannot have its way at the end of the day.
A cloudless sky as night passes by to wake to
another dawn.
Endless dreams, moments to savour.

Glad to be born.

Places - Hagg Wood

Jane L Wood

Along the peopled village streets;
Out past the playing swings,
Approaching now the broken wall;
The farmer's rough defence.
Step into the dark, still and silent
Hagg Wood.

Walk by the field-wall, just in case . . .
The horse safe beyond in the sunny space,
Is the 'hagg' hidden in the holly bush cave?
Is the problem lad about the place;
With his lurcher, his gun and
His kill?

Down through the earth pits; ancient wounds?
Down through the thorny thorns and burrs,
Down to the brown and busy brook,
Past the steep little slither - into the river!
To the dark stand of water at the weir head.

White with the sorrel and blue with the bell
Chill to the snow; warm to the sun,
Our young voices melt with eternal song
To fall through the trees,
And the years.

Still - around every tree stump and curve of the path,
Wind the memory ghosts of our personal past.

Where Love Dwells

Blanche A Carson

There's a place in my heart
For the woman I love
- A haven of peace,
No one can describe the comfort she gave me.

My childhood was sad,
Quite misunderstood,
Denied love, that I needed and craved
For a mother who cared
And a mother who shared
my interests and thoughts for each day.

This 'Mother' I found
Unique and profound,
Whose childhood was similar to mine,
Wrote books to inspire
Gave me the desire
To go forward and overcome pain.

The dreaded day when she died
There were hours I cried,
For the 'Mother' I loved and admired.
I deeply regret
That we never met
But felt her love deeply inside.

In Beaconsfield town
As I look around
And walk up the road near my dear friend's abode,
(Or a least where it used to be)
In sunlight's warm glow
As the gentle winds blow
Or waft of sweet spring in the air,
Re-assured at all time, her spirit's still there,
And her memory engraved on my heart.

A Sunday Sonnet

E M Tomba

Monday to Saturday I leap from bed,
Lunches to be packed and breakfasts are made.
A cup of tea to clear sleep from my head;
The plans for the day are already laid.
On Sundays I don't get up until late,
And breakfast is served to me in bed.
It's brought with my tea while I lie in state,
Crisp bacon sandwiched in crusty white bread.
Snuggled down softly, with room to spread out,
The breakfast tray pushed to one side, now spent.
This is the best part of that there's no doubt;
To capture one hour my only intent.
        Browse through the papers with leisurely pace,
        In all of the week here's my special place.

Bedroom

Stephanie Haley (11)

I have a little bedroom,
It's really rather sweet.
I have a little desk,
With a little seat.

I have a long thin wardrobe,
And a long thin bed.
And in the middle of the night,
I always bump my head.
You see, my little table,
Is really rather close
And when I twist and turn at night,
It's when it hurts the most.
It makes a bumpy, bangy noise,
And wakes up all the house.
But even if you're wide awake,
You know it's not a mouse

But you know my little bedroom,
Is really rather small.
It's cosy and relaxing,
So I don't mind at all.

Close Encounter

Bernadette Marley

What is it that makes friendship so meaningful?
It is the feeling of contentment, which results in peace of mind,
The harmony of spirit, which evokes joy,
The ease of conversing, which gives place to laughter

When, on a Friday, at the 'Carlton' in Leigh,
We order a gin and tonic
And sit down at table to await the toasted sandwiches.
Pleasantries give place to an opening of the soul -
We are lost in a private world, drained of self - consciousness.
The crockery and cutlery are placed before us,
we unfold our napkins;
But nothing can break the intimate bond forged between us -
The trivialities of the outer world are lost to us.

Yes, the decor is coldly classic, the dove grey
pillars complementing the blue walls;
A diverse clientele relaxes in its own peculiar way;
But in that eatery, called the 'Carlton', there is, for us -
A transient pattern of eternal peace.

Concrete Coffin

Charles Bronson

Like a tortoise without a shell
Hear the mad-man scream in hell.
Like an angel with a broken wing
A beakless bird can never sing,
Like a grave forever cold
Free is the soul it can't be sold.
Like a dream you float by
The old man cried until he die.
Like a shower of acid rain
It melts your eyes you go insane.
Like a bear inside a cage
A broken heart full of rage.
Like a corpse on a marble slab
You can't pay peanuts to a taxi cab.
The concrete coffin closes in
In a canvas jacket in the loony bin.
Madness creeps in through the wall
This is the place where Satan calls.

Dedicated to my 'Dear Friend'
Rosemary Kingsland.
Who has given me back my rainbow!

The Mine

S M Berry

The mine now stands silhouetted against the sky,
Dark and satanic - a poignant reminder of days gone by.
It's become a memorial for the souls that perished there,
Feeling no emotion - it does not care!

Yet once it symbolised hope and pride
And fathers and sons worked side by side -
To bring home a wage for clothes and food
'They won't go hungry - not my brood'.

But there was death and destruction within its bowel
An unseen enemy but just as foul.
The sound of the siren was dreaded by all,
Not just the wives and mothers but also the small.

Tragedy strikes,
The mine takes its revenge,
For the stripping of coal - there seemed no end
But over the years there was less and less.
Men laid off, with nothing to bequest
To their wives and children, save illness and disease
That unseen enemy that makes men wheeze.

The community suffers - there's very little money,
The traders leave this land of milk and honey.
Shops are boarded and bars are closed,
All that's left is the abandoned fire hose.

But the mine remains as a constant monument,
To those who suffered and died as a consequence
Of working and living in such bad conditions
As the dark damp dusty tunnels with their deadly emissions.

The Back Of Beyond

Kerry Appleyard

There lies the deep red sea,
That waits calmly for me.
Beckoning silently.
I will be free.
There shines a hazy sun
Of which I cannot burn.
I can wait my turn
In my presence alone.
And the sky shimmers in its softness,
While the moon changes in its quarters,
Whispering the importance
Of my present stance.
Standing in the beam
Of which I cannot be seen.
I await my peaches and cream
To guide me to my dream.

Talents

Caroline Gibbs (8)

Big or small
Fat or thin
In your body deep within
You will find a talent there
Use it gratefully
With care
Talents might be things you've worked
on
Maybe projects that you've learnt from
You may be good at seeking and hiding
Reading, writing, could be riding
You will get better if you try
If you get it wrong don't cry
Practice makes perfect
So it really is worth it.

Romance Of A City

J Woodhouse

It still retained its power,
Like a cat to the night,
Even though my dreams had long turned sour,
It drew me in as well it might . . .

I remember when it was all so gay,
The stores of old fashioned names retained their mystique,
But, that was yesterday . . .
Now in doorways, humble bodies reek.

Politics still dominate its river banks,
But the places of my youth have long since gone,
The seedy alleyways remain though, still curious, still dank,
The shoppers bustle onwards unaware and trundle on.

Now to me it was like a familiar face,
I look to its features and remembered the memories,
It had all been a tragic waste,
But I'd be back, one day, Somehow?

The Good Companions
Mary Young

A love of books,
A love of wine,
The beauty of a poem, line by line.

The shared humour,
The whispered sorrow,
The plans for to-day and tomorrow.

Love of sea
And love of sun,
Love of travel, food and fun.

Things of age
And elegance,
Happy trophies of the years' advance.

Love of quiet,
Love of ease,
Warmth and comfort, hearts at peace.

Close in spirit
And in thought,
Hearts and minds in love are wrought.

Love of God
And love of man,
Love of the future that our lives must span.

O Holy Spirit,
Flame divine,
Sanctify this love of mine.

That burning bright
And leaping higher,
It may attain our hearts' desire.

O Good Companion,
Friend of mine,
Did a Holy Cross our paths entwine?

Adolescent

Joyce Botha

By my bedroom window
In the time before sleep
In the years between child and adult
I would gaze out at the apple tree.
Its grey limbs darkened in the summer night
While its leaves talked softly to the light wind
The words ever just beyond hearing
What did they say?

Beyond the apple tree
The long garden glimmered
And stretched out of vision
Familiar shapes faded to strangeness in the shadows.
I feared yet longed to walk that midnight world.
What would I find there?

Beyond the garden, haze
Hung over the water meadow.
Within it dancers moved to unheard music,
Clothed in the moving mist, unrevealed.
Though I strained my eyes they were ever beyond seeing.
Who were the dancers?

In a clear sky
The moon rose,
Slipping between the branches of the little wood.
Free at last, its enigmatic light
Deepened the shadows and roused the owl to speaking.
What was the mystery out there beyond my reach?
When would I know?

Migration
Tim Hughes

The migrating herds of Africa
Of Wildebeest, Gazelle and Zebra,
Move forward as one spirit,
In their endless search for water.
They never question where it will fall,
Or know when they will drink,
But when rains fail,
When natures promise is broken
I wonder what they think?

Do they feel anger and betrayal
Those twin tormentors of the heart?
Or do they feel despair,
As we do, emotions torn apart?
Do they feel trapped and cheated
To be deceived so cruel?
Or do they feel forsaken
And left for dead like fools?

I wonder what their feelings are,
They surely never show them.
They guard their jealous hold on life
Until it's wrestled from them.
I envy them their strength,
Their acceptance and their trust
And I wished I could be like them.
And should you ever bless me,
Lord, then bless me thus.

The Trespass

Norah Green

Don't dare forgive my trespass here.
You left the door of your fine mind
Ajar and your soul's window-blind
I drew and trembled at its fear.

Then poacher-like returned again
To prey upon my gentle game -
But found it was myself I maim,
And crippled fled before the pain

Yet time shan't heal for time's a quack
So here's a fine old 'How-are-you'?
Far from well, as well you knew,
And stranded in love's cul-de-sac.

Go get your mental arrows straight
The facts are plain, the fiction purl.
This staid gavotte becomes a whirl,
Your bow's intent is now too late.

Now gone to earth, your love the gauge -
Nearer your dream, far from your bed.
Cool keep your sheets and clear your head -
A seal upon your heart, oh sage.

Sea Dance

Peter Kuck

I could say.
The sea is calm,
But was it ever?
I could say.
They've all gone home.
But then, some never.
Some stayed, and even now
Suffer the cold sea waves.
Not for them the warm return
To hometown graves.
How restlessly they move,
For they can take no stance,
But travel on from sea to sea,
captives of the dance.
Do they so far below
Save memories of the past?
If the tide was right
Would they homeward go?
For them the dye is cast,
Their tears have ceased to flow.
The rhythm of the tide
Their hornpipes will enhance.
And they will play with pride,
The dark, eternal, dance.

Once In Summertime

Katherine Wright (15)

The wind blows strong in the meadow,
my hair flies wild all around.
Like a wall the rain falls,
with my tears, pain and pride.

The stream runs forever
as do my dreams.
Always thinking of you
weeping under, the moonbeams.

Stomach links my heart
the pain of both inside
the love I had before
once in summers time.

In a summers dream
you and I lying
happy memories all around
now no love I've found

It all slipped away
like the stream still running
my heart lives for you
but you've gone with another.

I can think here alone
in the natural meadow
maybe tomorrow
I'll be strong, like the storm.

Paradise In The Imagination

R Peters

Paradise is a place where loved ones can go,
somewhere far away from the toils of life.
A place where imaginations can roam.
Two minds at peace, two minds as one.

Montreux

Martin Meadows

The lake is blue
The clouds are white
My mind's a misty haze
We walked past here some nights before
I wish now for those days

The mountains stand proud
The town is alive
The people are wandering too
But it seems the only thing on my mind
Is you and you and you

I love you
That's the reason
I love you
That's the why
I love you for all seasons
And I will love you until I die

Treading Water

Dorothy Farrant

Early morning on a calm, clear day.
Seabirds wheel and glide above the bay.
No one about but me.
Below the wall the wavelets play
As I give myself to the waiting sea.

High tide gently swells, embracing all,
My troubled mind is held in thrall
In the beauty of the dawn.
Yet today is my father's funeral
And my heart is anguished and torn.

Lost to me-the man I never knew,
Shy and reserved but strong and ruthless too,
Knit to me in tender fronds
Like seaweed, tangled, all askew.
Our genes repeat our earthly bonds.

Treading water, held in contemplation,
Sorrow and joy mingled in elation.
A small voice in my head
Tells me I have not lost a loved relation
But gained the whole world instead.

Granada

Jean Evelyn Mellor

Where snow-capped mountains touch the sky of deepest blue and
the heat of the sun
beats down to scorch the earth where the people toil and laugh and
pray
beneath the Sierra Nevada
Here in Granada

Where the hour is nearing twelve, some peasant women walk at
dark with their babies
sleeping in their arms. They look with sorrow in their eyes and trust
to pity as they
seek the tourists' money
Life is harder
Here in Granada

Where church aisles are painted in wonders of gold. Where people
hold their church
most dear and are keen to share what little they have
from a meagre larder
Here in Granada

Where saringo smells and lizards crawl, where donkeys work from
dawn to dusk
bearing their master's load. Where the pace is slow and thoughts can
drift to home
I think of you
Here in Granada

Carefully

Mikela Conboy

Touch tenderly, as I have given every fibre of my body to you,

Kiss lovingly, as I will return your loving kisses,

Embrace warmly, as I have embraced you,

Speak slowly, as I can drink in every word you say to me,

Walk slowly, as I will walk with you my love,

Hold me tightly, as I never want to be let go,

Yet tread softly as I have laid my dreams beneath my your feet.

Be Still And Know

I Spence

Oblivious to the time of day
Not a sound but for my heart beating
The room so warm like it's still May
The clean white walls with central heating
This aura of peace I have always craved
I knew for me, God the way had paved
That I'd be given the time to recourse
The wonders of His universe
Be still and know that I am God

Sister Madeline the gentle nun, her face aglowing
With such love and always knowing
That I am searching for what she's always known
And this peaceful convent is her home
nestling underneath the Big Orme
Like a trusting child in its mother's arms
And the sound of silence inside and out
Brings a thankful prayer to my mouth
Be still and know

To walk around this lovely place
So full of worship and quiet grace
Where the prayers of the endless years
Have wiped away my doubts and fears
Because I know there's more to life
Than jealousy, war, greed and strife
Seek ye first the father said
The sisters knew it and they did
Be still and know

Loretto of Llandudno, your heart is showing
Why do you show your beauty so
Glowing in your quiet rapture
Knowing how you hold and capture
The hearts of all who come and go
Radiating wonderful joy and peace
Like the sun rising from the east
You should be made a holy shrine
In my heart you will be mine
Be still and know.

My Favourite Place

Barbara Knight

My favourite place is in my dreams
When I am fast asleep
I need no aeroplane to fly me
Over oceans deep

For I can soar free as a bird
To where I choose to be
Where sands are warm beneath my feet
And I swim in an azure sea

I glide into the billowing waves
Down to the ocean bed
Where tiny iridescent fish
Swim playfully round my head

I touch the rarest coral
That man has ever seen
And the gently waving curtains
Of seaweed, emerald green

I seek out all the bounty
That the ocean has to keep
The priceless luminescent pearls
The treasures of the deep

I have no fear for I am safe
In my world beneath the sea
To shed my insecurities
And set my spirit free

When morning comes I wake refreshed
To face the daily chore
For in my heart I know that I
Can soon return once more

To that far place beyond this earth
Where time for me stands still
In my beautiful tropical paradise
Where I can roam at will.

A Hay Meadow Remembered

Bettine Symons

A woven coracle holds me
In gentle wave of dryland sea.
I muse, recumbent, here below;
Peer up at seed heads bowing low.
While cradled in a golden glow
Of stiff grass stalks, just ripe to mow;
So pattern, hue and symmetry
Is the fruitful grass surrounding me...

Sweet vernal grass, of golden hue
With timothy, dusted pink and blue.
And foxtails, just like a brush,
That sweep the air luxurious,
Donating odours light and gay
Redolent of the summer's day.
The quake grass snakes its nervous mop
Of rattling scales, prepared to drop
Its scattered jewels for next years crop...

And in between, the clover heads
Of mauves and creams and rosy reds,
Propagate extravagantly
Their nectar for the honey bee.
And oh! the summer symphonies
Composed by birds and buzzing bees,
And insects too and all that flies
Their song combine to harmonise
And soothe the earth with lullabies...

In this meadow, free of strife,
Earth is bearing gifts of life
That hum with gladness to be here,
Singing praise to the turning year.
Reclining here, on firm dry ground,
I feel the earth revolving round...

All life complete, where e're she goes,
Through summer heat and winter snows.
And I am one with the loving earth
Her lap, her arms, her giant girth
United thus with the universe...

Our derring-do has cost us dear,
we've made a poisoned wasteland here,
Where once this meadow, bright with hay,
Gave me such joy that summer day.

City Rain

John Grogan

Tears traced their soft film
Against your eyes
As the morning dew gently shimmers the grass.
Rain sprinkled its myriads
In your hair,
Freed to tantalising dance by the wind.
Darting streams stroked a pattern upon your face
Making a web of changing shadows,
And moistening your parted lips
To velvet wine.
With head uplifted in postural pose to the night,
You said in shrouds of mist,
'I love the rain.'
Incredulous anguish made me fear
To part such close caress.
I knew I was alone.

Spanish Interlude

Pamela Clarke

On wintry ev'nings when my husband's fancy turns from sex to sport,
Our kids upstairs begin to craze computer games of ev'ry sort,
I lock one door; foam mix my bath; then melt, meander southern Spain . . .

Hot, amid spires minareted, proud
While long palace walls stand shot through white,
Peering in courtyards bejewelled by light,
Fountains, - corners hidden from the crowd.
Driving down new highways, breathing broom,
Past mosaick gardens arched in rose
Where the lily-pools laze . . . on to snows
Dazzling views. Chillness. Does nothing bloom?

Chillness . . . I shiver slightly, flicking eyes, and gush the tap, again .

Hot, short-cutting southward, sweaty, bruised,
Catching Moorish ancient capitol,
Perched upon its rocky citadel,
As its apricot skies fall infused.
From the town, roads coiling up each hill,
Spring their grasses, Flanking floral weed.
Fields beyond afired. Once poppies bleed
No wild flowers tangle, overspill -

My door is rattled. "Mum, how long you be?" I pause. "Soon, soon, I think".
Still time for cowbells, faintly; such flamingo lake in chiffon pink!
I rise to dress; clean up my bath; then put away my past to drain . . .

A True, And Trusted Friend

David James Wilson

Friends are like the morning dew
That greet the rising sun,
And if they see you going down
They leave you one, by one,
But should Dame fortune chance to smile
To soothe your aching brain
Those fickle-minded, 'so called-friends'
Come crawling back again,
But the one who sticks, through thick, and thin
Right to the bitter end,
Is the only one you can really call
'A true, and trusted friend'!

The Château

Vera Riddell

Through gloomy shade of ancient trees
Where once the road was wide,
The course of years has let the ferns
Encroach on either side,
Sparsely dappled through green boughs
The track leads on its way,
Toward the distant arch-framed light
Out into sparkling day.

There stands the château in the sun,
Four square with pointed towers,
Encircled by its grey walled moat
And bright with vibrant flowers.

I stand and gaze; a lizard basks
Upon the sun-drenched wall
And in the hot still summer haze
I hear the children call.
Their voices waft across the years,
I see them at their play.
They'd hardly know their English 'Miss'
If they were here today.
Long gone are days when gingerly
We climbed into the boat
To feed the raucous mallard ducks
Who lived there in the moat.
Long gone the games of hide and seek
Up many a winding stair.
Do armoured sentinels today
Still keep their vigil there?
I hear cigales, as darkness falls,
Pervade the evening air
And on the moonlit tower, the owl
Who's silhouetted there.

So many generations
Have made their memories here,
Now mingled all together
They create an atmosphere;
Sweet-sad and almost tangible,
Each memory I trace
Makes this Medieval château
A very special place.

A Day At Langland Bay

Dorothy Osborne

Green and white Victorian day huts nestle in the curve
of crescent shaped bay, a jewel in the Gower crown
Picture windows, sparkling, perch on one side of mottled cliffs
A golf course, like lush green carpet on the other
Wind blown hedges point accusing fingers at the wind
A blizzard of seagulls swoop, wheeling, sobbing, gliding down
to a choppy sea, an armada of beaks and feathers,
Tourists relax, time to stare at any distraction,
Urging, coaxing, scolding children,
Empty bottles carelessly discarded lie like drunken winos,
Chip cartons, - miniature cardboard cities for sandflies,
Soon to be stolen by the tide as it ebbs and flows
The horizon is red, a flicker away from distant purple hills
A hump-backed ship sails across the bay, its scarlet stripe
stabs the eyes of fishermen silhouetted on craggy rocks
Frothy wetness slithers over beige sand, a rogue wave lashes
at isolated pebbles
An excited dog splashes into the sea; bathers cower from the
spray
A white triangle of sail cruises past like a paper yacht,
Beyond, a motor-boat zooms away with water-skier tail,
A monster kite dives menacingly and a child's laughter sends
it soaring, pigtail wriggling and squirming
The sun sets; the beach abandoned
And the lonely gulls wail.

Katie

Laura Edwards

Passing by one would not have given you a glance,
But when you came to stay with us, by a mere chance,

We were to find our lives had been completely changed,
You had somehow our circumstances rearranged.

We had become light-hearted, cheerful, delighted,
As though by some miracle no longer blighted

By cares and worries that had been getting us down.
They made us dismal, fed up, caused many a frown.

While you were amongst us the atmosphere altered.
We were pleasant, compatible, no one faltered,

Intent on keeping it that way, happy and bright,
Rising above their problems of which they made light.

You were helpful, assuring, kind words did you speak,
Nor was it in your nature gossip to repeat.

Friendly and sunny, a blessing to have around,
Some one who in this life is seldom to be found.

Lovely and fresh, not having yet attained your noon,
You were like a flower coming into its bloom.

We knew well enough how we would miss your beauty,
And begged you to stay though you were called by duty.

But there were others, one to whom you were mated,
Wanting your return. To leave us you were fated.

Silent were we, much diminished by your going,
Missed the way you laughed and spoke, all senses flowing

With the very joy of life, not a word in strife
Which troubles all too many, everywhere is rife.

I shall miss you, more than most, every single day,
It can never be the same now you've gone away.

Because of how you were you had stolen each heart,
Sadly empty our lives since you've had to depart,
The house so dreary again without your sweet smile.
Oh, Katie, please, do stay yet a while.

The Island

M Williams

Many a star-lit night, brings fond memories of a flight.
To New Zealand, a pre-paid holiday, a six weeks' stay,
Reunited with my brothers, an emotional, happy special day,
A dream which finally came true.
New Zealand's autumn colours with scenic views, were breath taking and beautiful too.
I panned for gold in a fast flowing stream,
Discovered flakes of gold, real, not a dream.
I climbed a mountain in shades of dark velvet green,
A Falcon, poised on balanced wings, screamed.
At Taiaroa Head was an Albatross colony,
In separate nests, two chicks dozed, unperturbed and solitary.
Moeraki boulders are huge spherical stones,
And emerge like giant heads through surging foam.
In Queentown by Lake Wakatipu,
The stillness of blue water flooded my soul,
Bringing harmony and serenity on which to hold.
Weeks flash by, sadly the holiday ended.
I'll always miss my brothers, their families, everyone so kind,
But New Zealand enchanted me,
The distant shores of the land I left behind.

Where People Like To Be

Angela Brennan

For some, to be alone,
Is where they like to be,
For they like peace and solitude,
And stark simplicity.

Some shun the life of humans,
Preferring animal company.
For they return the love and trust,
That's where they love to be.

Some, lose themselves in books,
In music or in poetry.
To be in life once removed,
Is where they like to be.

But for me the midst of people,
Is where I like to be.
The titillating, scintillating
Infuriating, aggravating,
The endlessly fascinating chatter of people.
And me.

Blind Man's Bluff

Dennis O'Brien

He makes us laugh, and is thinking all *day*,
You, can never, credit what he's going to *say*.

He can pull the *wool*, over anyone's *eyes*,
If you didn't know him, you'd have a *surprise*.

And when the driver, reverses the *bus*,
He shouts, it's all clear, and makes such a *fuss*.

And when the girls just strap him *down*,
He say's your beautiful, and he's no *clown*.

And when there's a word written on the *board*,
If you spelt it wrong, you stupid *toad*.

So close your eye's, and what can you *see*,
And are you all, thinking the same as *me*.

He can't tell the difference, between *night* and *day*,
He's a man of courage, I've got to *say*.

He, *is* to us like a *ray-of-light*,
And we all can imagine, what he feels *like*.

Hospice

Patricia Stamp

How bright the sun
How full the moon
The day has gone all too soon

I go to bed and pray for the dawn
Then once again a great new morn
Where does it go before too long
We're back and ready to see the start
Of a brand new day here in our heart

As I sit behind these door's
And gaze out on these beautiful lawns
The peace, the tranquillity never fails
To lift my spirit like ship with sails

The helpers here are all so kind
The nurses, cleaners, helpers all of one mind
To help people in this tranquil place
To keep their dignity and their grace

God is here and in his wisdom
Hand picked all those that here do come
To help the sick and lonely one
To carry their illness with love and peace
Till they enter that beautiful place

A place that all deep down do fear
But in our souls graciousness does rear
A face of beauty and of love
Care and serenity all around, someone always to hold your hand
No one here need be afraid
A path of love is already laid

A Rest In The Country Nearby

Garry Saunders

The water by the old fence where the cows seek shade,
Has begun to get cold as the light starts to fade,
And the whistles of the Shepherds in far away fields,
Causes me to reflect upon the joys that life yields.

Overhead the wood pigeon calls loud and clear above,
About me the bees buzz happily in their labour of love,
Whilst silence calls me to a land of dreams and rest,
I dare not close my eyes in case I should miss the best.

For high up in a darkening sky the stars shine bright,
They beckon my thoughts to wonder at their dancing light,
And as clouds roll by the scent of rain fills the air,
But warm and sheltered I can look on without a care.

Each leaf of every branch that whispers in the tiny copse,
Tells of the rumours from the farmer's ripened crops,
With their gentle murmur as they bow to the noble breeze,
I listen intently to the music of my ancient trees.

Here and there I catch the sound of a fox sloping by,
A wary rabbit pricks up his ears as he catches my eye,
I expect that the badger will cross by again on his trail,
The water-boatmen exhausted have decided to set sail.

I never once knew a night like this with so much to see,
I have sat here many times but the trouble was with me,
For I had failed to notice the beauty of the life I live,
But now I begin to realise just how much life has to give.

The Malvern Hills Remembered

Margaret A P Quinn

Oh I have walked the Hills in mellow autumn
When misty sunshine colours every glade.
Trod woodland paths, golden with enchantment -
Weeks of delight, before the colours fade.

And I have rested on a craggy summit
When orange sunsets blazed across the sky,
And heard the buzzards' wild and lonely calling
As they winged their leisured progress up on high.

And I have heard through a dusky twilight,
The screech owls eerie, haunting call,
And felt the calming stillness of the evening
As nights shadows reached and covered all.

I've felt the Hills reverberate with thunder
When summer storms have raged across the sky.
Have caught the awesome camera-flash of lightening,
And seen dark and tumbling storm clouds racing by.

Oh I have gazed at velvet moonlit heavens -
Seen stars like sparkling jewels suspended there.
Have traced with joy the many constellations
Awake and vital in the pure, cool air.

Oh I have seen dark snow clouds gather forces
And watched in awe a strong white blizzard rage.
Have felt its power, and heard its mighty roaring -
A daunting force that no-one could assuage.

And then have wakened to a clear, still morning
To find the Hills transformed in pearly light.
Have trodden then on snow-packed hidden pathways
And marvelled at an earth so pure and bright.

A Childhood In Gwent
Ronald Manley

Full three score years and more have passed since I,
Together with my brother, roamed for miles,
The leafy lanes and rippling rivers by,
Through grassy fields, by hedgerows, over stiles,

We had no cycles, could not take a bus,
We used our little legs, like grown-up men!
Our parents entertained no fears for us,
Nor did we fear - the world was safer, then.

We walked the towpath where once horses towed
The barges laden with wealth newly-won;
We walked where Roman legions proudly strode,
Their helmets, breastplates glinting in the sun

We gathered chestnuts in the forest glade,
Admired the banks of primroses in spring,
Laughed at the music by grasshoppers made
And even heard the songs birds used to sing.

We played at ducks and drakes in Ebbw's stream,
Black with the dust of coal from valley tips,
Or watched real trains, the sort propelled by steam;
In Campbell's paddle-steamers went for trips.

Each night I walked my sister's dog, alone,
Around St, Woolos' church - my constant rule.
Not from fraternal duty, I must own;
Here, Elsie Jones got off the bus from school!

I loved her dearly, never spoke a word,
Adored her from afar in secret awe.
Could anything be truly more absurd
Than one's first love? or ever matter more?

But now, the peace of an idyllic scene
Is rudely shattered by a motor-way.
Have poets, artists in these purlieus been?
What would they think, if they came back today?

As noise and petrol fumes pollute the air
And drive away the creatures God has made,
Who now can risk the time to stand and stare?
He'd perish with the fauna, if he stayed!

Now terraced houses climb the mountain range,
For people must be housed, the planners say.
Has progress not the right all things to change?
Then what the Lord made green must turn to grey!

At Powerscourt

George W MacMahon

In a torrent, cascade roaring
Down, on down, wild water pouring
O'er the ledge, in freedom falling
Through the moss, like silver soaring!

Streaming with a mighty gush,
Smooth the rock and onward rush,
Fill the air, a bracing flush
Grips the bones, the Soul to brush.

So, brush on by, but leave behind
A brighter flame, and peace of mind,
To banish trouble, cares unwind;
O! Waterfall! Most perfect kind!

The Smiling Gent (Grandad)

Graeme Lander

I would sleep in your arms
You telling me stories
I, taking it in through my subconsciousness
Your hands so large
So strong, yet, soft and caring
Never raised in anger
Never a wrong word spoken
Never a wrong thought or deed
The smiling gent
Never a frown
A vacant look
Always in another time and place
A traveller by right
The General's General
Now you travel with ease
One day, once again
I will travel in your arms.

Going Home To Mother?

Karen Edwards

Leave to be with you. Secure within the bubble.
Your messages of love sing loud.
The heart races to beat simultaneously,
The water of life pumps in anticipation.
I'm travelling to the light. Mother leads,
Her presence over-whelms.
The radiance from above, the fire mountain,
Calling me to you.
They followed the light, she lead them.
The rustic amber. The start, indicator of the day to follow.
Shine, speak loud sweet mother, so beautiful.
Let your message be heard.
The back-drop so unique to me it seemed.
Carrying me, so safe to you.
You told her to keep me, guide me,
To follow me with the beautiful journey.
Your words spoken, your touch light up the sky.
My beliefs so isolated, yet my perfect world would
Be shared among those also aware of mother's presence.
Each interpretation so personal.
Yet mother is the common thread,
Her colours flow into the night.
Her presence leaves me now as she reaches new horizons . . .
. . . And I reach my horizon, still perfect.
Stay with me mother, continue to guide me
With your precious fire
Goodnight sweet mother, rest now for
I am safe.

The Clent Hills

Moss Westwood

Once, in trauma, I found
My mountain to sit on
Terra firma; Solid ground

High on a lea
On the airy Clent Hills
Allowing me time
To ponder my ills

I go there no more
In times of duress
Wherever I am
Can provide mindful rest
As long as I can take the time
To transport my mind
To that lea on the airy Clent Hills

On Parting At Heathrow

H M Liebeschuetz

‘Go quickly and don’t look back’ parting is not sweet sorrow.
Parting is pain. Cut it short. Think of tomorrow.
New country, new people, new work, new landmarks to see.
These are the things you must think of. Don't think of me.
I will fill up the space with small duties, find tasks to do.
My pride and my love will sustain me when I think of you.
Now is the depth of the winter, the worst of the darkness and pain.
But soon there’ll be springtime beginning and planning to see you again.

Romney Marsh In Winter

Diana Jane Dean

It's winter on the Marsh,
And in the early morning air,
Herons wait with patience,
Beside the Dykes laid bare.

Swirling mists rise slowly,
O'er the vast expanse of fields,
The spires of ancient churches,
Are silently revealed.

Stillness, enwraps completely,
Grey, chilling to the bone,
In the distance can be heard,
The fog-horn's mournful moan.

Ducks and coots and moor-hens,
Lie sheltered in the reeds;
The sheep-dogs echoing bark,
Grazing lambs will pay no heed.

No place for the stranger,
Wandering, lost and seeking light;
A thick grey blanket now descends,
And brings with it the night.

Hope

Katherine Sharkey

It's three in the morning.
I'm sitting here on my own.
The thoughts they keep churning,
Unlike, starch in this uniform worn.

Most of whom are asleep,
In which my care they entrust.
The few that are awake,
Don't need much more than a touch.

So hence, I sit thinking,
In the form I know best.
In the hope that a verse,
Will help my mind rest.

Admittedly, I'm smiling,
Of what I don't know.
Of a look, or a feeling,
Of what I'm unsure.

To stop all that running,
To stand still and stare.
This is what is so unusual,
And gone is the pain, I did bare

There will always be doubts,
Or so I did think.
But now, I do wonder,
Who know maybe they'll shrink!

I do still have hope,
This I did not give up.
My life line, in front of me
But now - is it touched?

Untitled

Miranda C Shipley

I hold your face in my hands,
the blackness and the beauty,
enough to spin my head.
Being there, by your side in bed,
close, and cuddled with no cares.
Need to pinch myself for the awareness,
the whole night, sheer bliss!

I hold your face in my hands,
kiss the eyes that see so much,
and touch you, your body feels great
I'm in a state of oblivion.

Fire

Sarah Jones

The golden corn with ears of fire, swayed gently in the soft, summer
breeze
The poppies bowed their heads, and chattered excitedly with the
field mice
Their soft, rustling words were carried on the breeze over to the
Shiny red combine in the distance.
The bees were holding house-parties on the petals of the wild daisies.
Supping up nectar and occasionally chasing the brightly coloured
butterflies around in happy circles.
The chirping of the birds, was interrupted by a soft echoing rumble
in the distance.
The combine was on the move.
The summer breeze stopped.
Autumn began.
The poppies faded
The bees flew home, and the daisies lost their dignity and lay in a
crumpled and withered heap on the dirt.
August came and went, and the combine took the corn from the field
with its savage and snarling jaws.
September began and with it came the faint yet distant smell of
burning
The forgotten ears of corn struggled valiantly to rise again.
The smell of burning grew and grew.
Smoke filled the air.
Anything living was choked immediately
Suddenly, came the flames sparking up from nowhere, a blaze of red
and yellow, crackling, laughing like an evil witch.
The ground shimmered in the heat.
The roasting flames tortured the corn.
The fire burned itself out in time, but it was too late,
The charred remains lay scattered over the hard, hot ground.
The stubble was blackened.
The horizon was darkened by the smouldering remains of
what was once the golden age.

Midnight On The Promenade

Dean Griffiths

It's midnight on the Promenade,
After a night of whisky and smoke filled bars,
Thumping bass exchanged for whispering terns,
Neon for stars,
From claustrophobic clubs,
To wide open space,
Cool south-westerly winds, caressing my face,
Looking out dazed,
Upon a shattered glass sea,
Where a million moonlit spirits dance,
I find myself caught in the oceans trance
Tar torn lungs, breathe in new life
My aching head begins to calm,
The once chaotic sands lie still and empty,
But, for the carnival huts and imported palms,
There is no one in sight,
Everybody has gone home,
And for a few drunken moments,
This special place, is my own.

Gilgal

Dorothy Eadie

'Home at last', he told his folk,
That mighty man of valour;
'It was worth it all, the strain and stress;
We've reached the place - the place of rest'.

For many years they'd travelled
And their leader forty long,
A journey of a lifetime,
For some an age too long.

The memories were bitter
But to some a great release;
Egypt was behind them,
Ahead, a land of peace.

But now they'd come to Gilgal,
And here they took their rest;
The past can be forgotten,
The future faced with zest.

A place of preparation,
Memories and care;
God blessed his chosen people
And united them in prayer.

So much took place at Gilgal -
Joshua learned the way
To conquer the land of Canaan
And be guided day by day.

Soon they'll leave this place
And settle tribe by tribe;
The land they've dreamed and worked for
Lay West of Jordan's side.

Cannan - yes the promised land
And a longed for life ahead;
But uppermost in many hearts
Is Gilgal, the place of rest.

Love's Embrace

Kathleen E Leeson

The arms that held me then, still hold me now.
Perfecting all the long years through
A softer, gentler, sweet embrace.
Warm and familiar, tender - true,
His arms create a very special place.

Young arms of love, impatient, urgent, strong,
Ignoring change have mellowed and belong
In their familiar place.
Softened with age, yet still intent -
His arms surround, secure, content.

Our progeny have braved the world,
The years have flown, life's flag unfurled
Against the winds of time.
Pearl, silver, gone and soon the gold.
His arms are still to have and hold.

The Stairs

Bernadette Morris

The door was oak and inches thick, at centre was a lion,
grotesque and black, it mouthed a ring entirely made of iron
beyond this door a hallway stretched, gloomy and foreboding
it made me falter, as a child, with senses overloading.

No daylight ever entered here, no windows had been made
only the light switch by the door could make me unafraid
to walk the length of this dire stretch and thus to gain the stair
but even there I was not safe on boards so stark and bare.

The stairway creaked on every tread with a moaning kind of sound
I often raced up all six flights, not daring to look round
to see which ghosts I'd wakened with this haunting symphony
their chilling breath and grinning skulls, clawed hands that reached
for me.

I knew that if I dared to stop, or even worse - to fall
then ghostly hands might catch me - if they were there at all.
You see, I never turned to look in all my childhood years
so afraid of what I'd see, I failed to face my fears.

Even though I'm old and grey, I still have odd nightmares
in which I never reach the top of endless creaking stairs
I always wake up with relief, so very glad to know
it wasn't real, and now I'm safe in my tiny bungalow.

Honeymoon In Yugoslavia

Betty R Winbolt

An ancient castle, scarfed by snow-capped hills,
That nestled in a valley by a lake,
Was our sweet haven for two timeless weeks.
Beneath blue skies we walked the meadows there,
Bestrewn with wild flowers, bright amid the grass.

The mem'ry of it now with longing fills
Our hearts. If we another trip could take
To that Arcadian bliss nostalgia seeks,
Could we recall the magic that once was?

A war has wrecked this loveliest of lands
And bigotry and hatred had their way.
We found love there and beauty, gentle folk
Whose way of life was simple. Tell me, pray,
Did they begin the strife that killed their joys,
Destroyed their peace, their lives? Did they have
choice?

The Sea

Sandy Luscombe

Blue and green and sometimes clear
Calming or a force to fear
Such power untamed
And endless stories famed
Where battles were fought
And history was sought
Where love tales unfold
Which transported souls
Where treasure sunk deep
With secrets to keep
Where fishes are caught
Slaves transported and bought
Ever swelling
Always compelling
Dark as night
Beautiful in light
The power of life
Storm and strife
A yearning constantly in me
Forever drawn to the sea

Absent Friends

Chris Dore

Gazing at the old stone cross
With its long list of the lost
He stands in line, it seems like hours
To lay his wreath of crimson flowers
Heads bent as one in solemn prayer
The Last Post, lingering in the air
Then slowly makes his way back home
For once again he is all alone
From a silver flask, he fills a glass
And drinks to absent friends.

God's Masterpiece

Ivy Balch

The sea stretches from shore to shore
As far as the eye can see.
The sun beaming on the waters
Make twinkling stars appear on the sea.

Never ending rolling waves
Such a vast tempestuous sea,
The beauty is in its strength
So powerful -yet so free

Its ever perpetual movement
Continuous the ebb and flow
So beautiful the sea around us
And in the silent depth below.

As the tide comes in
It makes for inlet, rocks and caves
Sometimes like a mill pond
Or huge mountainous waves.

The ocean so full of energy
For ever it will be
Under Gods' wisdom and control
His creation, His masterpiece, the mighty sea.

A Perfect World

Kirstin Hodgkinson

Let us escape and begin to wander,
Let our thoughts begin to ponder.
Peregrinate into the infinite depths . . .

A different tangent.
A different reality.
Insanity?

Where money does not matter,
Does not clatter.
And there is a key to every door.
And more.

In a world of imperfection,
There is only one perfection,
For myself and each other to forever roam.

My special place,
In the human race.
That special face.
That I can truly call my own.

Those were the days,
And are the months.
And will be the years to come.

With no cloud in the sky,
No sun in my eye.

I am feeling quite high, on happiness.
Peacefulness.
Togetherness.

My thoughts rule my imagination,
Rule my mind,

Rule the way I act,
Where I go.

In my head is the perfect everything.
The perfect cure.
The perfect place.
To be and see.

The world is what you make of it.
Whether real or in your mind.
Your kismet is what you'll find.
In the depths of that kind.

In your mind.
In the depths . .
The depths . . .

The Fish River Canyon, Namibia

Peter Hutchinson

It's grey, dark grey, before the dawn, the sun has not lifted its head,
The vague shapes move while loading packs, no sound, and nothing is said.
The Canyon lies in darkness yet, deep shadows and near to black;
All we can see is an edge, then space, a void, but there lies the track.

The cars drive off, the first ray strikes, we bath in an orange glow.
We move to the edge and look over, but still it is dark below.
We stand at the sign very proudly, 'The Start of the Hiking Trail
85 k's as we're photoe'd, but inward we quiver and quail.

The sun arcs up, the deep turns grey, but shadows are still too strong
Emerging, through, the shapes and forms, the track we'd step before long.
In fright, delight, in fear and glee, we gaze in a kind of awe,
We hardly believe the width and the depth, it frightens us to the core

Let's start, one step, that's all it takes, and forcing our feet down the drop,
We inch and shuffle, stumble on; and, grasping the rock and rope,
Descend so slowly, foot by foot, the Canyon walls so steep.
The Canyon walls, of rock and scree, five hundred and five metres deep.

Still cold, but warming, movement helps, at last we come to a ledge.
Sink down, off packs, a drink of juice, we rest far below the edge.
We must stand up, we must proceed; how hard it is just to stand.
With aches and groans we lift our packs, our muscles are ours to command.

The path now eases, flattens out, our legs shake no more with fear,
The air is warm, the sun shines down, the river below is so near,
The reeds are green, the water blue, this seems just like Paradise.
My friends all smile, but I think aloud, 'There's 81 k's to Ai-Ais'.

At The Hermitage

Maureen Crampin

Old oak beams exposed and rare
Gems of bygone age
Symbols of a way of life
At the Hermitage.

Scent of roses round the door,
Olde world charm,
Feeding hens: collecting eggs,
Fetching milk from farm.

What's for dinner? Rabbit pie?
Treacle/apple pud?
Roasted pheasant? Cherry tart?
Bet your life it's good.

Smell of oil lamps: candle glow,
Warmth of logs ablaze,
Chestnuts roasting round the fire,
Time to sit and laze.

Crickets chirping in the hearth,
Kettle on the hob,
Home-made bread and cakes for tea,
Flap-jacks! Just the job!

Blackbirds singing in the hedge,
Nightingale in tree,
Swallows circling o'er the barn
Plain for all to see.

Days of camping in the spong,
Cooking on the fire,
Fetching water from the well
We didn't seem to tire.

How I loved those childhood days
On my Grandad's knee
Hearing tales of long ago
Learning history.

A place I'll long remember
In that 'golden age'
Memories of happy days
At the Hermitage.

Simply Home

Sonya Fay Manning

When driving mine no. 55 down to Peckham,
Ah de West-Indian conductor all de way
from de Caribbean feel mine 'hole soul
driving home in de warm winds cooling
de strain-o-mine mind sensing de deep
scent-o-falling green oranges, quenching
mine homesickness wid dier rawness wanting
to dance wid de side plate-o-fry fish ana
roasting breadfruits . . .

Always driving home hearing voices calling mine
name calling me to come down on de verandah ana
pass time wid beer ana rum - we simply ice wid
cubes from our neighbour Phil, whose only one
to keep a descent quality fridge ana inside loo . . .
Sweeter that de outside latrine running wid
tings that make mine nose snort up ana curse up
'Ingland bad me here still still driving home
driving just hoping to pay de bills de hp on
time . . . Just driving just driving hoping dere
would be no racial discrimination today . . .

Just driving home driving to make up
money to fill me belly to yam me breadfruit
ana yam dat get me tinking get me dreaming get
me driving me right home again . . .

Tulloch Moor

H Hepburn

A place of enchantment full of grace
Little trees all edged with lace,
A sea of purple meets the eye
Enhanced with sun from an azure sky.

The winding road goes on forever
Even the birds sing out their pleasure
Little creatures hop with glee
What joy! This heather rhapsody.

My Ship - Portugal 97

Deirdre A Lewis

There lies a ship in the Bay of Sunrise
And light glints on the furls of its sails.
The sea awakens with whispers and sighs
And greets the sand with its smile.
There is the hush of the early morn
And the world has turned in its sleep
There are no sounds of voices
Such still lie in the blankets of sleep,
Only the stirring of the mournful sea
As against the shore it weeps,
For the rest of the world
Is lost in its dreams, to lie
On the borders of sleep.

I can hear the wind and its sayings
It has soothed the night away
And the dawn of the day has touched me
In its very special way.
Dawn's promise has arisen
The sun, the sea, the sky,
It all lies here before me
I can touch it if I try.
This glowing world of promise
Embraces me in gold
The day has now awoken
And its mysteries shall unfold.

(for Anne)

2.44 On Glastonbury Tor

Rosemary A V Sygrave

Why am I resting on Glastonbury Tor,
seeking solace, inspiration and peace?
All my troubles, I need to ignore;
all my tensions, I need to release.

Beauty and peace surround me;
all my cares are far away.
Under the welcome shade of the trees
I sit, reflecting on my day.

For many years I longed for this;
- the magical, mystical, healing air:
'Twas well worth the wait; - such bliss!
Glastonbury's spell is beyond compare.

Once more I've found my own little patch
amidst the tourists on their trail.
From everything and everyone, I am detached.
Oh, this is such a joyful tale!

I've yet to climb right up the Tor,
but I'm rested, now set to go.
This day has been well worth waiting for,
so I want the world to know!

The Park Of Our Childhood

S J Prince

Four of us running through gates open wide,
Past grandstand and bowling green waiting inside,
Down pathways and grassways we charged our mad way
The park of delight in those halcyon days.

Green hedges, like mazes, impeding our flight,
Flowers in borders all standing upright,
Dark corners, light moments we shared in our youth,
A moment of triumph, a second of truth.

Park keepers, others too, shared our domain,
Dogs straining leashes to join in our game.
The grinning old horse that we rocked with all might,
Bumping of roundabout, swings that took flight.

We scrambled through undergrowth, planned strategies,
Sharing our youth with the ancient of trees,
Babies and benches and boys on old bikes,
Tearooms and tennis were for our delight.

Meeting in summertime, giggling gang friends
Starched skirts and white sandals, the latest of trends,
Radios blaring and secrets to share
As we lay on the grassland, beneath the sun's glare.

Discussed our tomorrows,
The days we had spent,
The park of our childhood,
The park of content.

Bournemouth

Eric Looker

Spoil now your senses,
Breathe as one pleases,
Privet and Pine, and healthy sea breezes,
Such beautiful sand.

Near Purbeck and Swanage,
The Old Harry Rocks
Like maidens in blouses or bright summer frocks,
Attractively stand.

Views of the Needles
Or the Isle of Wight,
Freshwater Bay's a familiar sight,
A nice place to land.

Sandbanks and Studland,
The sweep of Shell Bay,
Wide open sea where white horses play,
Such a fine coral strand.

Deer in the forest,
Clifftop and chine,
Five star supreme is a suitable sign,
Proud Bournemouth, -
Uniquely grand.

The Islands Of The Morning (At Henley Lock 6.8.88)

Frank Probett

Looked upon a sunlit river;
Rubbing sleep from out of eyes;
Can the day go on forever,
Watching dancing butterflies?

Every day seems but an hour;
Every year seems but a day;
And each single lovely flower,
But a dream along the way;

Morning mist upon the water;
(Can every day go on like this?)
And the heart-beat, -will it falter,
With a single loving kiss?

Even should life lose its meaning;
And the spirit issue warning;
I will take myself a ‘dreaming,
By those islands of the morning!

The Field

Betty Payne

I was a child about seven or eight
When I'd run through the lane to the
long grassed field
I'd kick off my shoes, on my back I'd lie,
And look up at the sky
I'd watch the cotton wool clouds float by.
Skylark swooped from aloft to its nest
in the field.
I searched, but I somehow never could
see
Where that place could be.
I'd stoop to pick the yellow Tom Thumb,
And get stung by the nettles that edged
the field.
The sap of a 'Dock leaf soothed the pain.
And I laughed again.
I laughed for the joy of being alive.
I danced through the grasses that grew
in the field.
The barley, the oat, and silvery shake
Would bend in my wake
There where the path was jagged track
I'd made my way back through the shadowed
field.
As the sun grew low in the rosy sky.
I walked on by.

Evening

Dorothy Staley

A hush now lies across the land,
Grey mist touches the brow like a ghostly hand.

The grass beneath ones feet rustles with a crispy frost,
The night owls call sounds like the cry of a soul who is lost.

A million diamonds fill the sky,
The moon casts her shadows as the clouds float by.

The wind is no longer loud or shrill,
All is quiet, all is still.

Nature has spread her cloak of night,
Darkness hides all from mans sight.

Enjoy the peace that evening brings,
For to us it gives release from mundane things.

A Place

Julie MacQueen

A place to hide, a place to retreat,
When all around the world does beat,
A throb, a hum - a constant drum,
What do we all become?
- Faces, hands, limbs and feet,
Each marking out our individual beat.

The sounds, the smells - the constant bells,
The twirling, swirling, rushing, whirling,
Such is life that we belong,
Working, fighting - being strong,
Constant deadlines overrun,
Is this life? - has it begun?

A place to hide, a place to retreat,
A place to stop the constant beat,
A door to open and close behind,
A place to rest our throbbing mind,
A place to find our inner force,
To delve deep into our very source.

To look upon a wondrous view,
To see, to breathe, to feel it too,
The simple beauty of a flower,
A tree - with all its strength and power,
A sky that rolls over vale and hill,
This is where life stands still.

No face, no sound - save gentle hums, of wind whispering from where it comes,
Of distant melodies of song, from birds above and far beyond.
This is a place where we may be,
Calm, serene, at peace - free,
To draw inspiration, to seek out light,
To face this world - with all our might.

Untitled

M Reid

Touch my fevered brow with your coldness
The pain, the intensity.
Is it fever or
The coolness of your hand?
No - more than this,
Tis the sweetness of a kiss;
Given with unselfish love.
This is the bond!

One Small Corner

C Evans

Small flowers and pebbles at its feet
The honeysuckle wreaths the fence.
Blushing to pink the tendril flowers
Waft through the house their heady scents.

Scarlet bright berries deck the stems
When autumn robs the year of green.
The birds like dainty acrobats,
From writhing stems their jewels glean.

No better place to rest my soul
Than musing in a garden chair.
With eyes closed on a lazy day
My thoughts can wander anywhere.

The dusty grandeur of the sphinx,
The marble nymphs of gorgeous Rome
Are not more precious or more loved
Than this small corner of my home.

Safe in content come niggling thoughts
How strife spews out the refugees.
Their special place, an exile's hope,
Lost remnants of their memories.

A Special Place - Derbyshire

Linda Brabrook

Peace quiet and solitude, in Derbyshire I look for you
A farmers cottage miles away from hustle and bustle
A place to look listen and hear the leaves rustle
Heron in the stream, sheep in the field
A farmer worrying how much corn it could yield
Matlock Bath old fashioned buildings and cable cars
Meeting place of motor bikers dressed like movie stars
Dovedale such wonderful scenery thinking it's a dream
A trip to a church flowers festival a riot of colour
Peace quiet and solitude
The lily so perfect looks like velvet only duller
Walking quietly in the Dales and Peaks
I'd be content and so happy to stay for weeks
My heart is healing even though I miss you so much
I found what I needed a special place to gather my feelings
Back in touch

A Walk In Virginia With Geoff

Pia Edwards

I long to walk the wooded path,
To smell the flowers, see the trees.
To take in God's wonders,
As honey is being made by the bees.

I long to walk the wooded path,
As the breeze rustles the leaves.
To feel that inner piece of mind,
Forget my problems, build my dreams.

I long to walk the wooded path,
To contemplate my years.
My hopes, my dreams, my failures,
My laughter and my tears.

Walk along a wooded path,
Sometimes when the day is done.
Forget about life's past few hours,
Find peace in the setting sun.

So walk along the wooded path,
Smell the flowers, see the trees.
Take in some of God's wonders,
And more at peace your soul will be.

The Eastern sun over the ocean,
I think of the path once more.
I long to walk the wooded path,
So much, no one knows.

Somewhere along these wooded paths,
A solution to my problem lies.
And if no solution is found,
Beauty still fills my eyes.

Sometimes beauty is the balm,
The eyes soothing salve.
We sometimes forget the beauty of nature,
We worry too much with what we have.

I dwell within the darkness here,
My eyes seldom see the sun.
I enter when the moon is high,
And come out when the day is done.

The Special Well In The Campsie Fell

Judie Mackenzie

They gathered in the mist-shrouded glen
To say their last goodbyes,
No tears this time, just silent respect,
No need to cry or sigh.
He was a brave heart, proud and strong,
A special man loved by all.

In the Campsie Hills - his favourite beauty spot,
To keep the well tidy, he endlessly fought,
And as his ashes scattered on the hillside,
Blowing in the vast and empty space,
They made this shelter his last resting place.

And when the sun rises then sets in the east,
He sits there smiling in eternal peace,
As the hawk soars high upon the hill,
He watches over his family still.
Looking down in the valley past the furthest city light,
His love for them burns long and bright.

So when you come to make a wish,
Or even just to quench your thirst.
You'll be kept safe in that grassy knell,
By the Guardian of the Well.

Rollright Stones

Carole Anne Johnson

I'm waiting at the
Centre of your beginning,
Encircled by your
Ancient strength.
'Speak to me,
  Speak to me,
    Speak
      To me,
        To me,
          Me.'
My eyes are closed
Flooding fire,
Shapes of surprise
Dance across my eyes.
A moon-washed sun
Soaks feebly into
The skin I wear,
A cooling breath
Plays in my hair.
'Speak to me,
  Speak to me!
    Tell me your secrets!
      Whisper to me,
        Engulf me!
          Give *birth* to me
            Here in the rain scented breeze,
              Before the hidden stars,
                Before the tiny creatures scuttling
                  Across your gritty surface.'
                    'Let the emerald life
                      Clinging to your crevices
                        Be my witness!'

'Bear me,
Lift me up to
Your soul!'

'Take me to the
Secret,
Make *me*
The secret!'

Seat Of Dreams

Raymond Powell

Here, in front of my home lies my
seat of dreams.
A stone slab with a view.
A view which cannot be matched.
My ideal world begins and ends
at this very spot.

As a boy, I used to sit here and
dream.
Sunny days brought warmth from
the midday sun
Filling my body with an
inner glow.

I could be anybody I wanted to be.
Do anything I wanted to do.
Go anywhere I wanted to go.
Nature would fill my senses
with an abundance of delights.

I could taste the air and feel
the wind on my cheeks.
Birds like sopranos would sing
and tell all the news of the day.
Freshly cut hayfields filled my
nostrils whilst baking in the heat.
Blue skies with white cotton wool
clouds could almost be plucked
with outstretched fingertips.

Nowadays, very little has changed.
My slab like a throne waits
to be sat upon.
The view of the mountains and
fields remains unspoilt.

I can still lose myself in my
thoughts and dreams.
This really is a very special
place.

Untitled

Tom Ginn

Do you remember as kids, along a pebbled beach we'd run,
through wet sand, to reach the sun,
take turns running, to pick up pebbles that shine,
you were only eight, and I was nine,
we'd always find a secret path,
and losing our way, we used to laugh,
then in the evening, the way home we'd find,
leaving sand castles, and sea far behind,
years later, we were older, and knew the meaning of love,
walking side by side, under stars above,
no, there couldn't be a happier time, than this,
when you asked me, to give you a kiss.
Love for each other, grew more and more,
as we walked along the sandy shore,
no more could you run and hide,
when one star lit evening, I asked you to be my bride,
we kissed and cuddled, my heart filled with happiness,
as you kissed me again, and said yes,
at a posh hotel, we planned to stay,
on our magic wedding day,
time has passed, and yet in vain,
I still wish, you and I were kids again.

North Norfolk Meets North Sea

Mary T Pegg

The whiteness of sand bleached by the sun,
dune grass tethered by roots that refuse to move.

Walking in water so cool and clear,
watching it roll and tumble over the shore.

The tide pulls and tugs at stones, shells and pebbles.
They go deep into the sand, hoping to be spared,
but the sea pulls relentlessly,
one more pull and it's back to the open depths,
the depths which ebb and flow forever.

A walk by the sea, a thought by the sea,
makes me see me more clearly.

My Favourite Place

Mary G Millar

My most vivid childhood memory
Is travelling from London to Durham by train
I went with my brothers and sister
To escape from the bombs that fell like rain.

We went to a colliery village called Brandon
The terraced houses were all owned by the 'Mine'
There were pit-heads not far from the houses
Bordered by a tanker railway line.

The coal heaps seemed to stretch for miles
But they never looked ugly to me
They were surrounded by clumps of purple flowers
That grew nearly as tall as me.

We watched the miners coming home for tea
Covered in coal dust from head to toe
They were always so cheerful and waved to us
They were the most wonderful people to know.

We visited nearby Durham City
With its splendid Cathedral high on a hill
The Cathedral has watched over generations
And I am sure it always will.

We picnicked on the grassy banks
Near the Mill on the River Wear
We stood on the bridge and watched the boats
I can picture it all so clear.

The river wanders through Durham City
Where its banks are shaded by lovely trees
I will never forget that childhood place
With treasured memories such as these.

Ring Of Promise

Carol Ann Luke

Strands of gold entwine to knot
The heart of the Celtic ring
Bare winter's finger unclasped its grasp
For seasons to marry those betrothed to spring
Yellow clusters of primrose promise
Tied together in a lover's knot
Celtic ring, sweethearts sing,
To bless spring's bejewelled engagement ring.

Snowdrops and daffodils together in a secret tryst
Winding in and out spring's garland
So hushed lies the secrets within each twist
Posies and garlands, rings of promise
Hold true the unspoken vows to spring
Plighting its troth to hope anew
For any who will pledge the ring.

Rings of friendship, Rings of love
Both precious gems to hold
The intricate knot of each unwind
Secret crocks of gold
Just as the seasons turn, every spring unfolds
A cluster of gold that rests upon the finger
A cluster of gold that spreads the ground
Shows the promise of spring season
When love was once before unfound.

Just In My Mind

Frances Ryan (12)

When the gloomy day is over,
And the world stands still for another night,
I'll close my eyes for natural darkness,
That makes my life seem slightly bright.

At any time, I can simply float,
Away from my life and all the lies,
I just place myself into a dream,
And all I have to do is close my eyes.

And in my mind, if I'm on my own,
I can silently call out your name,
As it's only in my special dreams,
That I'm in your arms again.

When I reach out I can touch you,
Your warm body next to mine,
Although you are not really there,
You've grown in my heart, through time.

I can block out all those little things,
And the tragedies with you,
Just the simple things you don't think about,
But everyday, you do.

The air that's full of coldness,
With a pinch of winter chill,
That dances off the condensation,
That lies on the windowsill.

My friends in the high street,
That could be strangers for all I know,
Icy memories that could be melted,
From just a simple 'hello'.

My special place was drawn out by me,
Like a perfect world placed in my mind,
I can just close my eyes, and be where I want,
Somewhere nobody else can find.

The Pathway Home

Hèlène L Tresadern

Through the corridors of our minds,
Through the valleys, deep entwined,
Atop the ridge of mountains high,
Almost touching the clear blue sky.

Below the oceans deep and cool.
Through the seaweed, a sunlit pool,
Below in caverns deep and bare,
Cold grey rocks are hidden there.

Through the forest of tall, tall trees.
Past the hives of the honey bee's,
Onward to a field of hay,
Passing the brook along the way.

Still further we go to a beautiful lake,
One that no earthly being could make,
Down the path to a house of grey stone,
The door opens wide and we know were home.

The welcoming fire in the old black grate,
The kettle stood boiling on a hob of slate,
The table all laid with mom's tender care,
Yes, we're home, and I'll never leave there.

Smile

Roger King

Happiness will come from sorrow so let your tears flow.
Watch the teardrop fall in a captured moment onto parched earth,
And from this wonderful gift, with a golden ray of sun, a seed will
grow,
Giving way to the fruit of Gia's womb.
So let the tears flow and happiness will follow
As sure as the life giving sun rises,
And the stars whisper ancient tales in the night.
So from this beautiful happiness the corners of your mouth curve up
to the heavens,
And share your big smile, everybody, because it radiates happiness
to all who are near you.

Remembering A Family Garden, With Swing

Betty Duberley

There are bees around the roses
on this day in middle June,
and the cuckoo soon will fly away
to sing his other tune.
In this green and golden garden
no human sounds are heard,
just the tinkling of the windchimes
and the whistling of the birds.

But the watcher at the window can very well recall
when children raced about the grass
and sang behind the wall,
there were shuttlecocks and scooters, near the lavender
in bloom and toboggans left in snowdrifts
on winter afternoons.

Yet all summer, into autumn, on to winter,
through to spring, the most favoured of the pastimes
was the crimson painted swing.

Now the watcher at the window is remembering with pain
how they lowered down the wooden seat
and laid aside the chains,
for the one who loved to swing there with vivacity
and power, lies now within the churchyard,
in the shadow of the tower.

How the colour of the paintwork fades away with passing
time, almost veiled by climbing roses meeting tendrils
of a vine. Yet trailing fronds and tracery
from baskets swaying there,
remind the watcher at the window
of a child's cascading hair.

Ode To Northern Ireland

Carolyn Hall

In the midst of the woodland glade
I breathe its purifying air
and I am assured this is the place
where dreams are made.

For in alien lands it lingers on my mind
poignant and distressing
but then I remember its people
and a hope you will always find.

Through crimson-stained streets
it does still remain and darkness
has prevailed in the tormented towns
where beauty and beast meets.

But in this place you will know
a warmth which would ignite the granite spirit
speak to me of no tokenism
this is my home - for all its lows.

As I journey through life far and near
I will hear it whispering in my soul
and my heart will in unity confirm
there is no place like here.

Morning

Dorothy Athorn

Away from crowded places
This morning's quiet solitude,
Reflects the joys of nature's mood
Blue the sky and noiseless cloud
Not a stir from any faces.

Silent yet the grasses tall,
Quiet time before the breeze
Bestirs and whispers to the trees
'Ah summer is here' to love and greet
The sun, that lovely distant golden ball.

Tender leafy clover flower
Still and pearly from the dew,
Unopened are the foxglove, with their rich and purple hue.
Transparent are the butterflies, as fragile wings unfold,
To lean against the silence of the early morning hour.

Dear Is The Land
Thomas I MacKay

Dear is the land where I was born
 And dear my native soil,
Brave were the folk who made her great,
 By grit and honest toil.

Dear are its mountains and its glens
 Its rivers and its hills,
Broad are the seas that leave our shores
 And wise our seaman's skills.

Dear are the creatures of my land
 Who share my native heath,
The birds that fly high overhead,
 And those that graze beneath.

Dear are the scenes of golden days
 Of summer suns and flowers,
And dear the scenes that greet my eyes
 Of winter's awesome powers.

Dear is the God who shields our shores,
 When tyrants rant and rave,
Strong is the grace that girds our lives,
 And great His power to save.

Dear is the land where I was born,
 However far I roam,
No place with thee can ere compare,
 Scotland my happy home.

Snow On The Christmas Mountains

Michael Lyons

The 12th month of the year has arrived
with snow on the Christmas mountains
a winter wonder, a ski surprise
with snow on the Christmas mountains
in the valley down below
where night reveals an earthly glow
the winter folk stock up with coal
with snow on the Christmas mountains.

An ivory sprinkling of magic falls
filled with seasons greetings
whiter than white and freezing cold
come the seasons greetings
in the hope of festive cheer
in the homes throughout the new year
the winter homes will prosper here while
filled with seasons greetings.

Now the land is glowing bright
with beauty and with wonder
as nature makes this home a sight
of flowers growing under
colours show and change their ways
and blossom in the summer days
a warm and light becoming phase
the beauty of the summer.

Once again the children play
in golden fields of autumn
playing games and rolling in
the golden leaves of autumn
in a breeze that comes around
slowly getting colder
feeling warm, protected from
the cold they feel in autumn.

The 12th month of the year arrives
with snow on the Christmas mountains
a winter wonder, a ski surprise
with snow on the Christmas mountains
in the valley down below
where night reveals an earthly glow
the winter folk stock up with coal
with snow on the Christmas mountains.

The Island Of Sheppy

Paula Penfold

When the night has fallen, and the air is still,
and the mist rises from the sea,
when the noise of the day, has gone away,
then the isle holds a mystery.

When the night birds call, and no shadow's fall,
then the mist comes rolling in,
in the stillness there is magic, the magic of day's gone by,
and I can hear the sea, give out a ghostly sigh.

It sighs, it cries, for soul's gone before,
and for those who to its bosom have yet to come,
it heaves, it break's and softly takes the island to its self,
the cliff slides in, the sea has left another lonely shelf.

Now nature takes what is her own, as dry firm land, turns into foam,
oh yes this island is my home, her magic hold's me here,
the magic of all the good soul's I've met, whom in my heart, I hold so dear
many character's, and rouges from London, who decided to settle hear.

Oh my island of Sheppy, with Abbey high on Minster Hill,
mankind may well forsake you, but God and I never will
the noise and the bustle of town and city, I've tried,
but here in your peace, my mind can rest, can hide,
for you gave back, what the world had taken from me
you beautiful island of old Sheppy.

Your air cold and clean, every city dwellers dream,
they come to visit in summer, like a mechanical stream,
then you put your winter gown on, and they are all gone
and we are left to ourselves once more,
then in the mist and the rain, I'll walk once again,
along your peaceful lonely shore.

Endymion

Clem Hales

One beauteous eve as the sun sank low
The moon ascended pale with woe
And looking down at the quieted land
Beneath observed a gleaming band.
Majestic in might rose a hill whose side
Showed well how fruit and flowers bide
upon soft slopes and the neighbouring vine
Around the elm in love did twine.
Dark hyacinth, grape, and the waving fern
Did in their florid land sojourn
Whilst faithfullest friend of their sweet repose
In silent sleep, the soft red rose.
There steeped in scented arboreal ease
And solitude, the drowsy trees,
Whose wandering feet to the waters edge
Came eased with bracken, twig and sedge.
A breath of wind stirred the slumbering stream,
Gone the glow and the pale moons beam
Tenderly tossed in its dimpled delight
Giving to earth in early night.
The moons first kiss, as the tapering tips
Of the Tamarisk with her lips
Were brushed, and ever lengthening its stride
Across the stream, in splendour pied.
The soft light swam in the sigh of the trees
Ocean of gold, for the blind breeze
Had, as then not dreamed to intervene
With the illumine of she whose lean
From out of her bower of starry charm
Was featured in the water calm
Where reflection bathed her like the flower
Of day, that slept this golden hour.

Under The Bridge

Jennifer Bainbridge

The water rushes over the stepping stones,
Ever growing, ever flowing.
Noises of different tones,
Dashing, splashing.

This scene has lasted through time,
Never changing or re-arranging.
The water, the mud and grime,
Singing, tingling.

I paddled there as a child,
Innocent and dreaming.
I was meek and mild,
Skipping and jumping.

The otters swim and play.
What a sight to see!
They move about all day.
What a way to be!

The water rats slide in and out
Of the cool, clean river.
The heron and the kingfisher flit about,
Always hither and thither.

The water talks to the hanging trees.
Leaves and twigs float and bend.
I pray on my knees
That this scene will never end.

Japanese Lantern

Catherine G Crehan

Robin sits on the lantern
Surveying the wintry scene
With Wren, the smallest lodger,
Searching for pastures green.
Daffodils rise like a chorus
With bowed, yellow heads
The sun will draw them skywards
To be picked for bowls instead.
Snowdrops, crocus, bluebells-
A waving sea of blue
All flowers God made for the garden
With colours of every hue.
Delphinium, Aquilegia, Liatris
With rich, varied spikes
Guard the curvaceous border
With hybrids and weeds alike.
Autumn sees the Acer.
Turn from green to red
It will soon be time for another year
To put the garden to bed.
But Wren, the smallest lodger,
Sits on the granite stone
With Robin curiously bending
Searching for food alone.
The garden is four seasons
It changes but never dies
With wonders never ending
Reaching for the skies.

The Dipping Place

Joan Shotter

Gone is our childhood but not the secret place
Where we sat and stared into the cool spring water
Harts tongue ferns
Push through the stones
Where the two steps down
Allowed us to dip our toes.

This place we ran to we called our own
Quiet and secret like the pacts we made
Dipping the water from our cool place
Splashing it over our bony knees.

We sat on the steps dreaming and pretending to be
In far away lands across the sea
With knobbly sticks
We poked at the bubbles
And shifting sand
And tried not to hear
When we were called for tea.

I'm afraid to go back to the Dipping Place
The spring will be there
And the ferns
And the peace
And the bubbles
But the dreams will be gone
It may all seem too small
I'll just keep my memories
Of my special place.

Avalon

F M Stephens

The clouds cover the moon
Carrying you back to a distant time
Where love is real and lasts forever
Magic is in the air
You breath it -
Feeling it sink into your pores
Mystery surrounds you -
But you have learned all
Shadows play tricks in your mind
Leaves fall gently to the ground
Night begins to fade
A chill passes through your body
You are back
Nothing is changed -
Nothing is the same
A dream caught in time
Never free from the memory
Wondering if it ever happened
A voice whispers -
It does not matter . . .
Time goes on . . .
The memory only a fading haze
Deep in your mind
Youth turns to age
Age turns to death
The knowledge never told
Nothing is gained.

End Of My Line

Lesley P Rainey

I'm not asking for a miracle
I just need a little hand
a lift up
to get me out of this.

I am pushing it to the limit
as far as I can go
up no further
that is me all over.

I am sitting on the edge
one more step and I am gone
but it is like tomorrow
I will never see it.

Where My Heart Is

Pam Wood

It's said that Scotland calls one back
Time and time again,
To where the purple heather lies,
Carpeting the plain.
Back to the awesome mountains,
Their solemn peaks on high,
To castles, lochs and ceilidhs
And the magic Isle of Skye.
The splendour of the tartans,
The pipes across the glen -
All send their haunting message
'Will ye no come back again?'

Yes, I'll return to Scotland,
To the place I love the best.
It's where I'm really happy
In peace and quiet rest.

Down The Mill

Sarah Platt

And we picked primroses there
And sometimes if you were lucky there was a coloured one.
'That's a polyanthus', said Mum
And the kissing-gate let us in
To the old rail track
And there were slabs
Of concrete left from the war
To stop the tanks.
In Somerset
And adders, still, soaked in the Easter sun.
'That's where I used to keep Misty', said Mum
And we run
And we run
Just the birds and the sun
And the sun
And the sun.

Angel Of Eternity

Alan Powley

In command of my fate and destiny
I set sail through the Bounty of Love
A voyage crossing a world of enigma
In spite of stormy black skies above.

You are the breathtaking seas of the ocean
Graced with sweet serenity and calm
Enchanted by your timeless elegance
You sparkle with a free and flowing charm.

Unparalleled beauty of inspiring view
Like a shiny star or precious stone
You softly and unknowingly entwine
All these gifts so clearly shown.

I cut through the waves with caution dear
To fall, the coldness I might find
Resisting temptation and depths unknown
My Angel, can you read my mind?

To the wind-swept tides of eternity
Cast me away from this perilous place
And cherish my ocean, my love and be sure
To allow me to vanish without a trace.

The City

Irene Rose

When morning breaks across The Park - in New York
The joggers jog
The skaters skate
The wildlife scurries off to sleep - among the trees.

The City rhythm picks up speed - in the streets
The sweepers sweep
The taxis hoot
The frenzied drivers shout abuse - the City hums.

The trainer - shod commuters rush - office-bound
They Walk-Don't Walk
Green turns to red
The subway steps they overflow - the sidewalks groan.

Hotels disgorge their foreign guests - to the flow
From map in hand
To structures tall
They gaze at all the famous sights - so much to see.

Rich smell of food is in the air - all around
Hot dogs 'To Go'
Hash browns with eggs
The Breakfast Delis beckoning - to everyone.

Luxury stores their goods display - diamonds wink
All can be bought
Though at a price
Yet, beggars lie around the doors -with paper cups.

Manhattan skyline silhouette - at nightfall
The stars go dim
The neon glares
Old Broadway glitters, colours bright - It's Show-time now.

The rich and famous out to dine - in New York
The limos purr
The taxis screech
Champagne is bubbling at the rim - It's Party-Time.

Then on to Jazz-club small and dark -West Third Street
Spiralling smoke
In shades of blue
Mingles with moan of mellow sax - It's cool - relax.

When dawn is breaking, homeward bound - in New York
The taxis flow
Through tawdry lights
The City pulse beats on and on - no respite seeks.

Just A Simple Thanks

A G Dyson

I see the light of a new born day.
I feel the breeze, with the corn nodding
its head in sweet content
I hear the murmuring of nature alive
with its wondrous magic, birds on
high for those who look.
I sense the presence of a true friend
by my side.
With line through rod we find a
place, it's not much good, the winds in
our face
But there are many who would take our
place, but cannot due to some ill fate.
So thank you Lord for this day, we would
like to come again if we may.

dedicated to a dear friend of many fishing years 1977

My Escape

B Gregors

Fantastic! clouds I see
Shapes like horsemen of the Apocaly!
Persian magic carpet rides I take
Across the eternity.
In my escape, none enter into my
World, for I am far away, you see,
Can I return at will, be back in the
Same day?
Do you doubt.
A flight of fantasy to live without.
Never!

Why Have You Disappeared?

Judith Anne Hodge

Oh! 'Special Place' in England,
How do I find you now?
Amongst glass buildings, stifling streets,
You've disappeared somehow.

You once were decked with berry trees,
Wild hazelnuts I'd pick.
Beneath protective branches,
In summer heat, I'd sit.

And children gathered bluebells,
So safely in your wood.
The hollow oak they played in,
So proudly, once, it stood.

The winding stream's forgotten
By all, save but a few.
Tots, trapping tadpoles in their jars,
Are just a memory too.

'Sticks'-thrown from rustic bridges
No longer is their game,
Replaced by 'Electronics',
All very much the same.

No picnics in your woodlands.
No birds nest in your trees.
Is this the start of things, to come?
Don't let that happen - *please.*

That 'Special Place' in England
Was 'my place' when a child.
Just moments from my Mothers house,
A 'feast' of all things wild.

You're 'Landscaped' now, in concrete.
Your streams no longer wind.
Your flowers, set in plastic tubs,
A sign of modern times.

I see only the beauty
Of all you were before.
On smoked-glass 'blocks' and 'robot chips'
My mind has closed its door.

What Is Your Favourite Song?

Vince Speck

It is invisible,
        creeps through the air,

into your mind,
what will it find,
        let it take you
        let it guide your mood
        lost in time
        what will it find.
A new century of pleasure
the real fortune teller
        passages that seem blocked
        instantly come unlocked
play that tune again - it sends me
        hope I'll meet you there.

Memories Of Venice

Beryl L Lambert

It was cool autumn when we went flying,
Climbing above our modern day traffic.
Leaving the gaping shores and winging,
Towards the warmth of the blue Adriatic.

How welcome the scent of oil and honey,
The wide vista, graced by vine and tree.
A land, steeped in the magic of history,
That folded within its arms, both you and me.

We stood as lagoon waters lapped the shore,
Lost in wonder at its pulsating motion.
Watching the water-boatmen ply their oar,
Seeing the sun catch fire to the ocean.

Gliding in a gondola, past damp palaces,
Under stone bridges marbled and carved.
Stopping at points where the canal interlaces,
Listening to the ribald, riposting, badinage.

Then magic moment, within a quiet waterway,
The sound of a gondolier singing a song.
Drifting on air, an echo from far away,
Leaving a memory that will live with us long.

Garden In Provence

Margaret Hanner

In the day, movement and light;
Sun on the water: insects in flight
over the pool in its frame of trees,
Their leaves astir in the summer breeze.
Heat shimmers on field and hill.
We alone are still.
Sounds recede: colours fade:
We lie and dream, content in the shade.

In the night, enveloping all,
Owl in its flight, dew in its fall,
Darkness, as far as the world extends,
Blackness around us that never ends.
And yet, and yet, to the watching eye
Appear the stars of the northern sky,
The Milky Way, the line of the Plough,
Long forgotten, we trace them now.

Night and day, ageless stand
Immense skies over ancient land,
We watch in wonder and delight
The tapestry of day and night.
This garden will be ever ours
With memory's unfading flowers,
Sunlight and starlight, lovely yet.
And we shall not forget.

Don't Want

Mark B Smith

Don't want a seat below the blue skies.
Don't want a part of the dream in your eyes.
Don't want a real, palatial mansion.
Don't want friends to encourage me on.
Don't want a place at the dining table.
Don't want to achieve what I'm able.
Don't want to snooze in front of the fire.
Don't want to play with dream and desire.
Don't want to find a place here to rest.
Don't want to pass the intelligence test.
Don't want any piece of this world.
Don't want to want,
when there's nothing to earn.

The Attic

Joan Leigh

The house is very old and weathered now.
It seems so empty, deathly quiet and small.
Yet as a child I know not how,
it felt so warm and safe and tall.
A haven in those far off days.
The steps are worn where once a welcome rang.
Through the rusty gate my ageing eyes now gaze
where still the rambling roses hang -
far reaching to the attic, once a magic place
of make believe on wintry days so bleak.
We played at dressing up and tig-and-chase.
Told fairy tales and tired of hide-and-seek.
Family portraits gathered dust upon that attic floor
and as the years past by, I wandered through them all.

A little girl, in dress of blue, white lace and pinafore
smiles out at me as if to say, 'you surely must recall
the picnics on the purple hills, the lightly scented heather.
The wooded walks, the stepping stones along the babbling stream'.
Those long warm summer days now gone, stay in our hearts forever.
A later picture, full of fun, recalls a merry scene.
A Charleston dress I loved so much and wore with charm and grace.
The feather in my hair no other girl could ever match.
No careworn frown, no worried lines dare touch this youthful face.
I must leave now, but as I turn to close the creeky latch
I see the cranes, the concrete blocks, so high one cannot see
the hills of purple heather or the gentle rippling streams.
So let the house be gone. It has no further use for me.
For I, like time, move on to build my life with happier dreams.

Waves Crashing Upon The Sand

Daniel Baker

In the dark I sit there scared and wild,
Upon the same rough stone steps, the same land
I joyfully played on as a young child.
Watching the cold waves crash upon the sand.
It's cold. I can feel the wind, hear its song,
Stroking, battering each side of my head,
I'm still holding on, but doing it wrong,
I can't forget those things you did and said.
They're still there, the memories, of those times,
And how we were like simple lyric rhymes.
I remember how I promised a friend
I'd see this life out to the very end.
But this life can't hold me. I'm crying and
Watching the cold waves crash upon the sand

Australia

Margaret Naylor

How beautiful this land I love
the rolling hills their beauty
changing hour by hour.
Gold at sunrise, green by day.
But when day dies
and dips behind the hills
night comes quietly
but -with what-glory fills the sky
purple gold pink
colours unbelievable.
My heart is full.
But will the image fade
and die as years go by?
Or can I recapture
the rapture of that beauty,
in paint at least?
When I pick up my brush
and dip into colours
mixed with bright Australia sun.
To paint a memory.

Ten Tors

Anna Walker

Oaks and sycamores, birches and breeze,
Makes the only place for me.
Loved and lost and found again,
Always witnessed by beloved ten.

Summer warmth through your stone,
Warms my mind - I'm not alone.
Winter snow blankets you,
Then I know - you miss me too.

Spring showers soaking call,
Brings me back for answers all.
Autumn winds whip us around,
My one and only stomping ground.

Your majesty will never cease,
Nowhere else can give me peace.

Stable

Beatrice Gwynn

In Bethlehem, passing, a tourist by,
He said, There, look what I spy!
There in that stable rugged and torn,
I on a mild December was born

My mother averred at my birth
Did a star shine, almost settled
On our roof, like a pigeon, an angel;
And my father at Nazareth,
'Twixt sawing and hammering.
Recalled odd strangers -
- We were there some days -
Gifts they left on departing,
A chunk of gold
For the baby, they said,
Perfumed oil and frankincense
For my parents,
For grieving, they said,
Their blessing they left; but the best,
Said my father, were shepherds
Curious come the baby to view
With pastoral eye: 'Like a lamb'
They said, 'He sleepeth, that's good'
'He'll be a shepherd too in his time'.

He laughed, a young man passing by
A ruined stable with a tourist eye.

Later, when all was said and done,
His mother passing by, in woe and tears,
Confirmed the story to listening ears;
But the stable had gone when they returned,
Not a stone remained of a spot so dear.

In other stables, re-used, forgot,

The lost stones lay by the common ones
- But shone out at night, as mica gleams
Out of dull rock, like a star re-born.

The Confession

Elizabeth Mary McNally

Slowly, silently, stealthily, I push against the heavy antique wood,
And all at once a sudden change comes over my present mood,
Dare I, a sinner, enter into such a place of good?
And yet I do.
But not proudly, or confidently, 'though I wish I could
But my sins - they are not few.

Like a thief in the night I tread softly on the ground,
Entering silently, and gazing all around,
My eyes rest on a wooden cross, and upon it, a figure bound,
There hangs Jesus.
The nails and thorns which his sacred head surround,
He endured to save us.

One cannot imagine the suffering and the pain
Of his self-sacrifice for the sake of all men,
And as my wicked life I remember once again
I wonder, 'Why
In order to cleanse our souls of sin's stain
This man should die?'

A burning shame as I've never felt before
Sweeps over me now like the waves upon the shore,
And as all my sins, I remember more and more,
I weep bitterly.
For this strange, new, unfamiliar pain is sore.
'Forgive me'.

I whisper my simple prayer into the silent air,
But to meet those loving eyes I do not dare.
There is no noise, but in the hush I feel his presence there,
Radiating, vibrating, exciting me.
And the peace and comfort now is beyond compare.
For he has forgiven me . . .

Building Site

F W Leedham

Bright sunny morning.
Memories of former days.
I looked across the road
And saw elysian fields.
Felt tranquillity.
Now I look across the road,
See building site.
Through gap in hedge.
Dis-ruption scattered over ground.
Grey concrete blocks
Sprout over large area.
In between, ruddy stacks
Of bricks, strip bound,
Covers flap in breeze,
On hard, muddy stony land.
Made up roof frames, window frames
Lie neglected.
Soil and gravel form small mounds.
Yellow JCB's driven by
Yellow helmeted drivers
Lumber between obstructions.
In far distance.
Grass covered screen
Hides, dims
Heavy traffic - bright sunny morning.
Look across road.
See Building Site.

Wild Horses

P M Hanson

I dreamed we two were in a field one day,
Wandering like children through the tall grass
Uncaring, lost in this verdant pasture.
The sweet heady perfume of wild flowers
Invading and capturing our senses
With a kaleidoscope of memories.
Long gone childhood, mysteries and magic.
Time became polarised. A long second
Stretching like an enchanted bridge o'er space,
Infinity spanned it seemed. Filled with hope
I turned to you, already you were gone
Intent upon your own affairs, worlds away.
A small fear like a chill breeze ruffling the
Summer calm, caught me unawares, I sighed,
Yesteryears spell broken by today's grind.

Meandering through misty lanes of time
Tangled hedges of Sweet Briar plucked my clothes,
Like thoughts of time past, hindering my search.
Coming at last to a broad green meadow
Replete with lush herbage and running stream.
Far away I glimpsed wild horses grazing.
Suddenly, sensing my presence they moved,
Nervous, pawing the ground, sniffing the air,
Galloping soundlessly forth, manes tossing
Turf's flying, mad eyed, nostrils flared. Jostling,
Hustling, ascending now to soar like birds.
I knew then I witnessed a miracle.
And finding you seemed easy, there you stood
Close by. I called and pointed to the sky.
You smiled, came to me but saw nought above.
Awaking to reality and peace
I saw then the frailty of my dream and
Would remember the horses forever.
But knew nothing could recompense for love.

The Seat In Tor Woods

Howard Hubbard

Through that ancient clattery gate,
What's the time - am I late?
Up over Tor's slipping rocks and roots,
To the seat of yesteryear.
Will she be there to clasp my hands,
She, with long luxurious hair
In honey strands?
The twisting path, St Andrews Bells,
Mellow and comforting pine-woody smells;
So near
To the seat of yesteryear.

What then should I do,
As I sit on rusting iron
And flaking green paint,
Waiting for you?
Admire the view?
It's better than John Hinde beauty.
Seen by so many,
Admired by so few.
My Cathedral in September half-light,
Towers puncture a crimson sky.
And draw down yet another night.
All this
From the seat of yesteryear.

Oh, what beauty I cannot appreciate!
As I endure love's torture,
The endless, inevitable, pitiful wait.
What use?
Somehow I knew
That she would never show.
For our date was on this day
Seventeen years ago
On the seat of yesteryear.

Crosby Garrett Churchyard

Roger Hodges

Here among the quiet ones,
Each marked by still, still, stone,
Only breeze and pen moves
And I am all alone.

Looking to horizon,
Of Wildboar Fell,
And thinking, thinking, thinking.
Remembering so well.

Did Moses think on Moab Hill,
More alone than I,
For I hear tractors, chainsaw,
And sky-blown rooks' in raucous cry.

Cows below in valley bawl,
And slowly move toward the gate,
Waiting for the herdsman's call
And ration of their cattle cake.

Moses, he was quite alone,
Not a grave in sight,
Not a noise, except the scuttling,
Of a lizard on the stone.

Yet not alone, for God was there,
And angels too, to bury him,
On foreign hillside stark and bare
Away from friendly tribal kin.

Not to the land of Canaan,
But upward Glory was his way,
And at the end of funeral day,
One unstoned grave was his.

And only God
Knew where it was,
And is.

My Special Places

Linda Boon

There are many many places,
That hold fond memories for me,
Sun filled holidays in Cornwall,
The rugged cliffs, the azure sea.

White horses along the horizon,
Racing in towards the shore,
Lazy days in the sunshine
Sandcastles by the score.

The countryside is also,
A place I love to be,
Cornfields, poppies, cowslips,
The giant oak tree.

Watching ducks along the river,
My face breaks into a smile,
As mother is proudly followed,
By her ducklings in single file.

There is no single place on earth,
That fills my heart with pleasure,
There are many places I have seen,
Whose memories I'll always treasure.

My Wee Place

Timmy Taylor

I live in my wee place, you see.
It's not very big, but it's enough for me.
With sloping ceiling, orange and yellow paint,
Makes anyone who's mean or grumpy smile.
I love the bed of odd sized cushions,
But more than anything the deep carpet pile.
My needs are not more soft furnishings,
Curtains or even lights,
Because I can just spend my days
As anyone else would nights.
You curl up or sprawl and just doze,
Because, that's my ideal life.
Lie back, relax, forget your worries, trouble and strife.
Tucked up in here, I'm as quiet as a mouse,
While the children storm past at play,
Let's not get involved, in here I'd rather stay.
When the children play, they wreck my wee place,
I know! for me they like to include,
They always become rather boisterous,
And the children I'd rather elude.
Then there's my next door neighbour,
We once had an acrimonious affair
Which ended in much scratching and scowling,
When I criticised her ski jump nose
And long tatty ginger hair.
Now I must end by revealing a little secret,
That is, in my wee place I must always have my own way.
Because I'm such a grown up now,
I refuse to use my litter tray.

Achalader

Louisa McKay

My beautiful Achalader

Many years I walked your spacious halls

And played on your surrounding lands

Never thinking of the day I would leave you

But that day came and I cried

I was then told big girls don't cry

I have been back to see you

My beautiful Achalader

And like you I have aged

And yes big girls do cry

My beautiful Achalader

Poet's Paradise

Stephen P Fox

I scratch my head with my void fountain-pen.
Where is my special place?
Do I have one, I wonder? Do you? Picture

Illusions of joy and promise in your youth before
The fall of the rainbow society seen
In the snows of yesteryear: images
Romantiscied by the spectral window of nostalgia. A
Fool's pot of gold. Or do you vision

Being with your lover on a snow-white beach at sunfall?
Under a crystal sky tinted with distant violet hills;
Gaping at the golden globe which hangs like a
Glistening guillotine blade behind the sanguine horizon.
A clear sky is only
A sky waiting for tearful clouds to intrude: when
The storm arrives the lovers dispair. So

Do I. A special place: a place of eternal delight?
Preposterous Disneylands!

My special place; perhaps like yours?
Is here: at my bleak, black desk. Braced to
My hard blue chair, boxed-in
By sickly green walls. I restlessly
Probe my exhausted genius for a spurt of inspiration's ink.
A pitiful sight: scribbling
Fanciful, trivial bombast with hasty verve;
Seeking a solid solution to an insoluble ink,
Sheltered from outside where Sol
Beams a radiant yellow blaze over vibrant
Emerald fields; fields scattered with
Childish seeds of optimism which
Laugh gloriously in a dream innocence.

Where is my special place?
Do I have one?
                    I wonder . . .
I dip my pen in the spouting well,
It's all in my mind; is it not?

Love Is

Maria Chissim

The wink when no one else can see,
Hearts as one, yet spirits free.
Conversations without a word,
To always listen, and yet be heard.
Sharing the bath in the candlelight,
Making up at the end of a fight.
Sharing secrets from the heart,
Minds may differ, but souls not part.
Childhood honesty-always true,
To face a problem and see it through.
Breathless laughter and tears of pain,
Love to give, not just to gain.
Feeling sure, not think - but know,
Always friends and never foes.
Kisses so tender, so sweet and long,
Hugs that squeeze from arms so strong.
If love is all these special things,
Then love is what I've found with him.

My Special Place

Lesley Charters

I walk along the empty beach
With dark grey skies above
Giant waves they crash to shore
Scurrying to push and shove

The eerie cry of a sea-gull
Above the howling gale
Could that be a boat in the distance!
With a little white fluttering sail

The wind it whistles round my neck
My voice will hardly speak
The salty spray, it showers me
It's biting on my cheeks

Bits of wood and sea coal
Are strewn along the shore
Empty cans, and dead sea birds
Doomed to fly no more

It's winter in this special place
Of which I feel a part
No matter when I'm far away
I'm there, deep in my heart

Cityscape

Elizabeth O'Hara

I hate the city.

I hate the city by day.
An aura of smog tacked in place
by tower-block nails.

Faceless beaurocrats with suits instead of souls
trying to deny their own humanity.

Homeless wanderers who have had their's
denied them.

I hate the city by night.
Reflections of streetlights dancing like demons
over the black oily pavements.

Women selling their flesh on street corners
and with it a piece of their soul.

Gangs of boys prowling the streets, old enough to kill
and young enough not to regret it.

But the worst thing about the city is that you cannot see the stars.

Perhaps that's why.

What Wales Means To Me

Jessica Johnson

What Wales means to me,
Revolves around the sea,
Of all the beauty everywhere,
The bay three cliffs has made me stare.

The prominent three large points we see,
Are beautifully carved and sculpted by the sea,
The crashing waves convince my mind,
That there are treasures yet to find.

I simply sit among the rocks,
To ponder while the vast sea rocks,
Although green pastures beckon me,
No-one can escape the power of the sea.

As if in a trance I stand and stare.
As if . . . no-one can see me there.
Transfixed by the beauty of the sea,
That is what Wales means to me.

The Hills Of Wales On Holiday

B J

The week amidst the hills
Wonderful views and oh! so still
Peaceful sounds of animals and birds
Sheep and cows in their herds

The house martins, so many flying
The sheep in the meadows . . . baa-ing
Horses playing, nuzzling, lazing
Cows and their calves, grazing

The smells of which I am not so keen
Make my nose twitch. Whilst beholding this scene
The hills are alive, with their own music
I hope to remember, and never lose it

Through the cottage window I can see
The forbidding hills. The clear blue sky
Even the ducks upon the pond
All the scenes that meet my eyes
I am really growing quite fond

Strolling in nearby Abbey ruins. Thinking of the history beyond
Who walked the paths of yesteryear
Were they happy? Were they in fear?
They would never be aware, that we the future
Would be standing here
I truly wish I could retrace
The bygone people who lived in this place

Oh! every morning I awake to see
The breathtaking views all around me
How simply great to start the day
In such a really amazing way

Time is flying, the holiday will soon end
If I close my eyes, I can pretend
That I don't have to return to the rat race
That I don't have those problems to face
Yet even with the memories I hold so dear
I can hear myself saying 'What am I doing here?'

I know life is for living
Things for taking. Things for giving.
Experiences to measure
My holiday in Wales. Is certainly one I will treasure.

A Place In Time

Penny Wattingham

If there's a place where I could be,
Then it would be beside the sea.
Upon a cliff, while all around
Bright orange flowers do abound.
With the sun so hot upon my face,
Relaxing - easing life a pace.
Calm, blue sea and clean, white sand,
A silver ring on a thin, brown hand.
Barbecues on the beach at night,
Friends we made by firelight.
The summer song that we all sang -
Do Wah Diddy, by Manfred Mann.
And then, if I avert my eyes
Just to the left, I see a prize.
A harbour, and a cobbled quay,
Fishermen, artists, you and me.
If I could be the girl once more,
The one I was in '64,
I'd like one perfect summer day,
Just to live my life that way,
One of a crowd - a time in our lives,
A week in Cornwall - at St Ives.

The Calm Of The Sea

Louise Richards

Happy, contented, my spirit set
free,
I become someone else as I pass
by the sea.
Laughing and running, past rock
pools and crabs,
Life's suddenly fun and not nearly
so drab.
Exploring and splashing, and
flying the kite
Feeling at ease, with nothing to
fight.
Rosy and glowing, special memories
to keep,
Then re-living it all as I drift
off to sleep.

The Child

Beatrice Smithies

He stood absolutely motionless by the pond today.
The expression on his face made me stop my homeward way.
Bobble hat askew and eyes full of joy
Wonder and fun radiated from that small boy.
His arm still raised beside his head
After throwing to the ducks, some bread.
Watching the ducks clustered round his feet
As they pecked and struggled for something to eat.
His sudden shout of great delight
Startled the ducks into instant flight.
His smiling mother standing by
Said 'Come along, son, please don't cry
It's time we continued on our way
We'll feed the ducks another day'.
A wonderful, magical moment for me
Recalling memories of when I was - *Just three*!

To

D Savage

To look the whole world over
To cherish and to hold
To take it all for granted
To only be so bold
To realise its wonder
To accept all you can see
To watch all pain and suffering
To know that you are free
To believe you make a difference
To ask just if you do
To think there is a heaven
To ask a place for you
Too scared to know the answer
To wonder if you care
To see the ones you loved before
To imagine they are there
To hope your dreams are real
To trust your heart is true
To have a place in heaven
To find the best in you

That Place In Mind

Janet B Slack

That place I knew and loved,
We shared it, Dad and I, delighting in its secrets,
The first unfolding celandine, spring peeping, hedgerow dark,
Soft cushioned calyx in a burst of gold.
'Now spring has really come.'
He'd led me gently to this host of year
Climbing the lane from slag heap's gloomy pile,
His grime-worn hands soft-keeping mine.
The path was blackened, pit-boot hardened,
But at its sides what wonders, mysteries, thrills it nurtured
To my awakening eyes.
He showed me my first primrose,
And how to feed the new-born foal,
We watched the tiddlers darting in the dad-dammed brook.
He taught me how to stand on tip-toe on the bankside
To catch soft smell of honeysuckle or his Columbine,
He showed me bugs and beetles, tuned my ears to birdsongs,
And with me stroked the furry backs of wild things.
Heard with a saddening sense the cuckoo's final plaintive cry.
. . . And so much more, that this became our special place.

So often I returned, in all its seasons,
Saw summer's sunflecked dancing leaves,
Watched cows graze, lazy now in fading grass,
And browning brook's slow trickles disappear,
Hunted for nuts - there surely here were catkins!
And sampled yet unripened berries from the brambles.
But, with a whoop of winter, what a wonder,
A white cast hardened track of fun and frolic,
Sharing my 'place' with friends we sledged and tumbled,
Skidded and tossed with freezing fervour,
Racing down pristine hill to ice-cast basement -
In monolithic whitened splendour . . .

That place I knew and loved.
It still remains, its purpose changed - with progress?
The colliery gone, scant bird songs fill the air,
Few children play, enjoy and forage,
As green fields yield to man's inventions.
But memoried places best retain the best in mind
When seen through rose-hued memoried eyes,
May fade - but fasten hard that place in dreams.

A Walk In Caldervale

Janet Cross

Down in the valley, and over the bridge.
Past a row of cottages, that stand on a ridge.
With their neat little gardens full of colourful flowers.
That someone has tended, for many an hour.
Then along the path and up to the pond.
Looking out over to the ducks beyond.
Beside it the stream bubbles and gurgles its way.
Making its journey to the rivers and sea every day.
We carry on up through the trees.
Where a carpet of bluebells sway in the breeze.
Across the stream, grey squirrels play.
Soaking up the sunny day.
Such a delicate fragrance fills the air.
As we climb up the steep hill and pass the big pine trees there.
You can hear them whisper to the wind and the breeze.
Telling their tales of the seasons that have been.
Then on we climb up the hill.
'Til we come to a church all quiet and still.
A picturesque and pretty, architecture of work.
Quiet and peaceful with swallows nesting in the porch..
You can hear them chitter and chatter as they talk.
Oblivious to all the passing folk.
Tranquillity and beauty all rolled into one.
Blessed by the warming rays of the sun.
Next to the church, stands Caldervale school.
Where the children come to learn, play and abide by the rules.
The trees stand tall by the old school yard.
Just looking like soldiers, standing on guard.
Watching over the children when they come out to play.
Out on the field, on warm sunny days.
Then back on our journey we must now travel.
For the steps we have made, we must now unravel.
We read the children's poems that they have done.
Inspired by the places I have spoken of.
How lucky they are to live in this place.

Tucked away in the hills nice and snug, away from life's pace.
Back to the cottages that stand in a row.
Past the flowers in the gardens that bloom and grow.
Here our breath-taking journey must end.
Until the next time, when we return again.

A Favourite Place

Marian Acres

My favourite place
When outside there's snow
Is by the log fire
A warm friendly glow

So I toast my toes
In an easy chair
Then sneaking a doze
When nobody's there

The main fear I have
There is little doubt
If I'm discovered
I could be turned out

Not talking about
The cat, possibly
I'm talking about
The fact that it's me

Not fully furnished
The house that we share
I should admit then
There's one easy chair.

Karma

J J Turner

Does the tide sweep in
as the coming storm abates?
Do we twiddle our thumbs
and give way to our fates?
Does love know no bounds
bar the fences we erect?
Can I be party to your heart
or is there another to elect?

Ah, sweet is the juices of a lover's body
introducing false promises as insecure kisses.

Will we sign the latest treaty
to halt the cannon's roar?
Will we transgress the treadmill
take flight and soar?
Who watches over our gentle embrace
taking beauty from love at birth?
Who feeds our feelings with junk
to wrench hearts once solid in mirth?

Come to the arms of warm naked desire,
trust in communal souls interlocked.

Do you feed the flame of cupid's bow
to breed a knowledge for two to share?
Can I suckle the breast that temptation offers
hard and erect as we lie together bare?
Do you come to the drumbeat of lust's percussion
in the twilight of dawn's new day?
Can I secure belief as trust sets in
or hear all the longings you fear to say?

Hold all hidden dreams of secret desire
in time, every fantasy can come true.

My Church

Doreen Mayers

For 900 yrs it has stood there
Amid the chestnuts and the birch
Its mellowed stone ... majestic
My lovely village church

Sometimes my heart is racing
And the tumult doesn't cease
Until I reach my place in church
It's then I find my peace

I feel such calm when I'm within
Those ancient old stone walls
I sit so very quiet and still
To hear God if he calls

Often when I'm all alone
And almost drift in sleep
My mind just starts to wander
And I'm privileged to peep

At ladies in poke-bonnets
And stately crinolines
The gentlemen all stiff and starched
As they confess their sins

Then I see the little girls
Arrayed in snow-white dresses
Cute small boys in sailor-suits
All sporting golden tresses

Then two by two the servants come
Some rather grim of face
And to the back they make their way
Oh yes ... they knew their place

When my reverie has ceased
And I return to present day
My church, it seems quite ethereal
And to the Lord I pray

I thank him for my ancestors
Who built this lovely shrine
To witness through the ages
And to stand the test of time

Although . . . one day . . . I'll join these folks
Because time marches on you see
And will someone sit in this same pew
And will . . . that someone . . . think of *me.*

Nostalgia

Alec Dunsmore

The night leaps Westwards and long, palpitating
day
Gives up its searing hold, unending harsh
demands;
The first relieving breath of landward evening
breeze
Stirs the long pendant fronds of palms that
rim the surf,
Rustles the bougainvillea overhead and speaks
of ease.

Comes then the sweetest time of tropic day
That brief and blessed pause when work makes
play
(The play is more demanding that the work!)
When, as the swift, flamboyant sunset dies in
night
We can relax our tautened minds, our jangled
nerves
And drink the peace - and scotch - and
dream of home.

Long leave seems far away - nine weary months
to go -
The rains are due and night-humidity is high:
Depression spreads his pall on our unwilling
soul,
But not for long - soft-padding-houseboys'
watchful eyes

Anticipate, and cater for our willing need.
Soft stars are out, too soft, too languorous and
moist:
Far northwards some of those same stars burn coldly
bright,

Ice-blue, like diamonds in the winter sky of home.
Already, there, the winter evening has closed in
And from the snow-capped Bens austere, which
palely gleam
Like ghostly jewels in a frosted frame comes a
keen breeze,
Scentless, but sharp and clean - which this dank,
tropic coast can never know -
Down darkened glens whose black and sleeping woods
are gripped in frost,
To blur and dim the grey-blue surface of a quiet
loch;
The exile home again upon its ageless shore
Where distance, stress and transience all have
ceased,
And heart and timeless memory alone remain.

At Peace In A Chair

Shirley Fraser

Sit in your chair
Close your eyes, now listen,
I'll tell you my dream
To relax is our mission.
Just think of an ocean
Aqua and clear,
Curling over in rows
To sand, litter clear,
An island off the Gulf
Of Mexico - 'tis true,
Like a long thin ribbon,
And it's there for you.
Pick up a conche shell,
Put it to your ear
Smell the salt and harken,
Sea's echo you'll hear.
Hot sand at your feet,
Feel the sun on your skin,
Sense the tranquillity - and ask
'What world am I in?'
Birds swoop down, or just sit
Bobbing on the sea.
On the azure, glistening water
In motion perpetually,
Lift your face to the skies
The warmth enters your heart,
Makes you feel privileged
Now a person apart.
The mesmerising sound
Of the sea on the shore,
What else can you want?
There is no more
What cares did you have?,
They're gone with the wind
For now you're in heaven

With total peace of mind.
You are aware no longer
Of sitting on you're chair
For now, you are relaxed
On a cushion of air.

The Desert Island

C B Brown

Our secret holiday in the sun.
Was so much joy and fun.

No one else had to know.
My feelings for you I could not show.

Those two weeks spent alone in the sand.
Were worth more to me than a wedding band.

My memories of that time will never fade.
For it was then my love for you was made.

Gibraltar

Dorothy Baines

I have a very secret wish
To travel back in time
To when I was a little girl
And my life was so sublime.

A large ship took us across the sea
To start our lives anew
We settled in Gibraltar
Where the skies were always blue.

Although long ago, I remember well
Many a happy and carefree day
Secure and safe with my family
Content in every way.

When World War Two started
It put an end to our perfect life
Once more we sailed across the sea
Away from the trouble and strife.

Sadly we never went back there
I grew up and found happiness again
But to me Gibraltar was a special place
And fond memories will always remain.

Special Arms

Valerie Scott

Arms outstretched
She ran to me
How I loved this precious thing!

Eyes full of expectations
Ready for our fling.

Arms entwined with love
We cling to each other
Round and round we went
Granddaughter Megan 6.
And Grand Mother!

Just A Rose

I L Sherman

'The scent of roses always takes me back
To one day long ago when I was young,
A gentle lad gave me a rose so sweet,
And with it just a little snatch of song.
The moment passed (as moments tend to do)
And years have rolled on by -
With joys and woes,
I hope that life's been good to you dear friend,
And thank you for the rose'.

An Essex Estuary

Anne Bromiley

I will paint for you a water-colour in words,
of a wild landscape whipped by gales,
a narrow water course, winding its way
through creeks of smooth mud, topped by seagrasses.

A tidal water creating eddies of rhythmical waves,
flowing in undulating bands of pink, mauve and green,
the sunlight and shadow ever changing,
as the clouds cumulus and threatening, block out the autumn sun.

Multi-coloured boats curtsey on their moorings
wait silently to do their owners bidding.
Meanwhile an oyster boat chugs up and down
dredging in ancient lanes laid in Roman times,
harvesting a delicacy fit for kings and serf alike.

The sea-wall worn by many feet, steeply bordered
by brilliant green slopes neatly cropped, stretches
to beds of feathery reeds, a haven for birds
who diligently feed on the mud flats.

A feast of texture, colour and smells
Invade the senses, uniting the observer with the elements
An aesthetic marriage of instinct, familiarity and roots
endless sky, autumn colours, restless water
an unspoilt horizon of beauty, tranquillity and peace.

My Favourite Walk

M Stuart

For twelve years now, round the field I have strolled,
With my two faithful dogs, who are growing old,
Every day around half past three,
Before they have their daily feed.

In sunshine, rain, strong winds or snow,
They frolicked round, chasing to and fro,
But now we go at a slower pace,
No longer can they run and chase.

The field to many is just, mud, grass and trees,
In the summer full of wasps and bees,
Hovering about from daisies to clover,
With birds and butterflies gliding over.

Thirty minutes spent amongst natures beauty,
Then home again to do my duty,
Feed the dogs and prepare a meal,
But relaxed, refreshed and contented I feel.

Just a field, but to me a pleasure,
With such happy memories for me to treasure,
My dogs were pups when we first went there,
How many more of our walks, can we share.

They sniff the trees and blades of grass,
And whatever else they wander past,
One day I shall walk there on my own,
Yet in my heart, I will not be alone.

The Colour Of Contentment

Debra Walker

They do say that green is a relaxing colour,
how appropriate then that it should be,
the colour of almost everything natural,
the colour of every leaf and tree.

To walk through a wood with somebody special,
be it your lover, your dog or your child,
gives the most beautiful sense of well being,
and all of your happiness shows in your smile.

My favourite places will always be wooded,
where all of my problems just fade away,
and I finish my walks full of self knowing,
I'll be a much nicer person that day.

My Childhood Home

E J Whelan

Surrounded by fruitful fields
Shire horses; cows, whose yields
Provided milk; and yellow butter
Made by mum with utter
Determination and hard work -
Something our family did not shirk.
Ducks, hens, guinea fowl,
Turkeys - raised by mum, pigs galore,
Cabbages, rhubarb and much more.
We worked, we played,
Our parents worked and prayed,
We had our secret place -
Full of wild flowers, we'd race
Home from school for tea,
To kitchen smells - and free
We read or played ball.
On Sundays dad was a preacher,
Mum our Sunday School teacher,
Our home was 'West View Farm'
All the hard work did us no harm!

Helvellyn's Despair

B Marquis

Oh! how my heart is aching
my bones slowly breaking
from the weight of all those feet
tramp, tramp, tramp; advance and retreat.

From base to peak
the rape continues
week upon week
my shattered sinews
cry in despair
no human can hear or care.

Reports from the rest of my range
tell a similar tale
of behaviour to us so strange
from base grass to summit shale
a catalogue of wanton damage
on the Pikes, Lower Man and Striding Edge.

Why don't they admire us from afar
or go elsewhere, climb a distant star
for in time our very fabric will be no more
our memory embedded in folklore.

The Lesson

Helen Tingley

Bells ring,
Children run,
The day done,
New life begun.

Clocks tick,
Time runs,
Adults rush,
The pace too much.

Lessons past and present,
To be learnt by us all,
The truth hard on the person,
Oh! but the joy of it all.

Will we ever know what drives us,
Fate or fortune?
Love or hate?
The sadness and the gladness,
Of what we've known before,
Leaves us standing,
Alone with ourselves,
Reflecting the past,
And the importance of now,
The real lesson for us all.

Delightful Devon

Judith Stones

Two 'Yorkies' came to Ilfracombe,
To spend a holiday.
It took all night to get here,
For we live many miles away.

The scene from our flat window,
Is quite a splendid view.
There's the busy boat filled harbour
And the cliffs of Hillsborough too.

We took the cliff path to Combe Martin,
It's a bustling thoroughfare.
Our aim, to climb the hangman,
Well, we almost made it there.

Then, we 'legged it' down to Lee Bay,
So pretty and serene.
Just like a sparkling jewel,
Set into a ravine.

We called in at the 'Tea Shoppe'
Just by a little stream.
And tucked into a plateful
Of scones and clotted cream.

Inland to Berrynarbour,
'The Globe' there is so quaint.
With its pretty hanging baskets
And its walls of pale pink paint.

A bar meal and a drink there,
Then we are on our way.
Down the Sterridge Valley,
Had another pleasant day.

There are leafy lanes to wander,
Coves and cliff paths to explore
And the locals are so friendly,
We just could not wish for more!.

My Bedroom

Steven Smith (19)

What does it take, he slowly reflected,
For the past to be detected?
A scent on a pillow, a melody long played,
And my bedroom brings back memories long delayed.

The past as tangible as a taste,
My soul enthuses through these simple square metres of space.
A Beatles calendar, a pair of go-cart wheels,
A poster of Doctor Who and a youth already sealed.

A bookshelf of diversity, of growth and disposition,
Spine showing, face hidden and more, each an emotional passion.
A video collection, from C S Lewis to the saga's of Mulder and Scully,
A closet of ever decreasing space, packed with memories more fully.

Ghosts incomplete, resplendent in their imperfection,
Their figments only visible to my ethereal perception.
The angel light on Eileen's face, Duncan's snores echoing,
The cries and laughter of friends past, ever continuing.

Songs of time and emotion play out of fashion,
On a stereo from a Christmas of love and forgotten passion.
The Kinks, Dusty and a certain Lennon and McCartney,
Remind me of her and that night in January.

They remain frozen on a turntable of light,
While over near the window, a 17 year old bounces through the night.
A 12 year old lies on the bed, reciting his days journey for posterity,
While a 19 year old stands and smokes, yearning for her.

A million me's, in a million states,
In a million memories.
A million me's, with a million fates,
In a million memories.

And all from one, one place of pain and joy, rapture and doom.
That's my bedroom.

Lullaby

Lorna Todd

Sleep child
Whilst I spin a magic yarn from the night air
To weave dread dark into a loving friend
And wrap you in the spell of all my dreams

Cushion
Your weary head upon the softness of my heart
And rock against the cradle of my chest
My strong arms will enfold you with a love
That shields age-old night-demons from your eyes

With dreams
Eye-lids flutter and close
For here you have found rest
With limbs entwined in safety till the dawn

Sleep on.

Wasting Time

Angela Simpkin

Sitting day dreaming wasting time
Watching clothes blow on the line
Wishing that I could save up or borrow
Time wasted today, until tomorrow

When out for the night and time runs out
Only too soon we hear the 'Last Orders' shout
I'm not ready for home, why can't it be seven
Its gone too quick, it's almost eleven

And beofre I know it it's time for bed
Time to lay down my weary head
To recharge my batteries, sleep and dream
If I'd had extra hours, of what might have been

Equal portions measure this life of mine
Into seconds, minutes and hours of time
Time wasted today, forever lost with sorrow
Time I could not save up or borrow

Wales

Gary T Barton

Magic and mystery
Stones and serenity,
Wales and Anglesey.

Faerie glen,
A walk amongst the trees
Peace, strength, harmony

Streams and rivers
Mountains hazed in mist
Love on a lake,
Surrounded my enchantment
In an autumns bright colours.

Earth power rising
Life's dance spiralling
Dolmens and night
The magic of life.

Fair Day In A Ramshackle Town

Sheila Smyth

Ramshackle town, a rainy day;
A mucky earth, a sky of grey;
Remembering now that noisesomeness;
The cow-dung spatters on my dress;
The brutal stick ill-used to flay
A stubborn calf that would not stay;
Like her, I longed to slyly stray
From all the shouts and yells of this
Ramshackle town.

When I grew up, I ran away
From all the fairs and all the fray;
But now I want to repossess
My youth, and all that magic mess;
The time has come to cry: 'Touche!
Ramshackle town'.

My Adopted Home

Heather Feetham

These fenland sunset skies,
Floods of colour as from an artist's brush,
Stretch across before my gazing eyes.
Breathtaking beauty of my adopted home.

I've learnt to love this flat and furtile land,
Though once I yearned for hills and pastures green
You changed my life that day I took your hand,
Your name, your home, the love you gave to me.

High winds and storms can sweep with winters rage,
Unhindered over marshes from the sea,
But soon the calm of spring arrives on stage
With carpets of bright yellow daffodils.

Our love has strengthened through so many years,
Undimmed by worry, work, and failing health.
We've shared together laughter and some tears,
Loving for ever, our home, South Lincolnshire.

The Beach

Sue Peake

Tanned feet wander along pinkish coral sand
footprints washed away on the changing tide
as the palm trees bow on the cooling breeze
praying to gods of whom we know nothing.

The sun beams down with remorseless glee
turquoise, ever-changing sea shimmers in its glare
walk, dream, think; azure dreams of I, myself and me
- will I ever come back again?
If I return, will I too have changed?

I cannot speak, I meditate,
ignoring other people that I see.
The beach rests quietly now.
Am I really here or is this an illusion?
Wishful thinking, an island, a break
from the mundane mainland of life.

My footprints, reassuring, they are a reality
reaffirming my existence, I can see them
shapes of little feet firmly printed on the shore
but no, waves sweep in, they're gone,
can I be so easily washed away too?
That surely was an illusory proof -
if they can't exist, neither do I.

The ocean thinks not, nor does it care
for these petty humans worshipping its infinity
carelessly treading on its shore
believe in some greater plan,
a different place, a different time,
for my reality is no more.

Chaos

Lee Lowsley

Looking around the world to-day we do appear to have gone
Astray
The world has been turned into an unequal place totally
Confusing the human race.
Hoarding and greed is now leading the way regardless of
Knowing we have a short stay
We need to change direction so may I suggest a way!

A world without banks at all indebtedness would start to fall
The overdraft system is a snare by bankers forgetting who put
Them there
They charge the earth with supercilious force hell bent on
Pressurising their source.
Banks and accountants a professional pack, but disposable people
We all know that
When observing small businesses in flight they connive to pull
The plug overnight
Oh, for an amnesty for strangling them on sight.

Look to the alternative building society's portray
But they fare no better at the end of the day.

Then the money markets started leading the way with Barings being
Their protégé
Will the future herald their decline or are we placing our trust
On a live line.

Stashing one's money under the bed would outwit the parasites
Overhead.
Politicians are next in line we could feed the poor on their
decline
They milk the cow and don't feed the cat
A safe haven for crooks we all know that.

On to the religious leaders who stand as a shining light when in
a position to have a wife they take a mistress to
Brighten their life

The only conclusion I foresee is Armageddon being the key to
setting us free - to start again - woppee!

Relative Insignificance

Emeka Obiandu

Midway between two opposites-
the valley and the mountain top-
I am at once a giant and a dwarf.
He is dwarfed by me
That stands to my left.
I see his tireless body
reeking with exertion
in his unwavering resolve
his goal to accomplish,
my enviable height to attain.
Poor fellow!

I stand to the left
of who stands to my right.
To their left, all that stand,
are small and beneath notice.
Even his sunset shadow
is cast away from us.
From his niche of our envy,
the rest of us are in the valley-
the nadir of consequence.

Heart's Ease

Margaret E H Lenn

Where the crystal river passes
Late refreshed by summer shower,
Lowly couched among the grasses
Hides the tiny pansy flower.

High above, the fells are lifting
Mighty shoulders to the sky,
And unhurried clouds are drifting
Where the lonely buzzards cry.

Patterned are the meadows over
With the tapestry of May,
Bees about the crimson clover
Drowse the timeless hours away.

In the stillness, lambs are bleating
And across the silken lake
Comes the cuckoo's call repeating
Notes that summer's height will break.

By the peaceful water's kneeling
In the changeless mountain's shade
Pluck we heartsease for our healing
When a debt of pain is paid.

Memories Of Malvern

V W Lowe

Malvern is my home town, I've lived here all my life
From toddler to a school girl, teenager then a wife.
Actually born in Warwick not far from the castle walls
Where the peacocks strutted nightly, disturbing mother
With their calls
My family soon returned to Malvern and by the time that
I was one
My life in lovely Malvern had only just begun.

The hills are big and beautiful, the Beacon best of all,
We'd play around the Toposcope and really have a ball.
With my brother and my sister and our friends from Lower Wyche
We would climb straight up the
Beacon, never bother with the path
Breathless and excited, life was just a laugh,
There was a little cafe that sold cups of tea and pop
It really was a lifeline for those who reached the top.
The air was clean and healthy, the view beyond belief
With every shade of green from grass to tiny leaf.

We'd play down on the common where the cows and sheep did
graze
And the buttercups and daisies made a perfect carpet haze,
The boys would play at football, the girls at hide and seek,
Then we'd paddle in the little brook that gurgled at our feet.
We'd gather up some frog spawn and take it home with us
If mother missed her jam jars she never made a fuss,
Malvern was a special place no matter where you'd been
There was no where in the world to match Malvern's lovely scene.

I am now a pensioner, the years have simply flown,
Malvern hasn't stood still, in fact it's really grown,
The view from up the Beacon is not the same at all
There's still a lot of green to see but also wall to wall
I'm rather sad to have to say it's bricks and mortar all the way.
So time has told on Malvern, but love it I still do
With so many happy memories surely you would too.

Steam On The Track

Mary Lacey

Crossing the bridge by Kemps Eye Farm.
I look down on the track -
Oh, how I wish that someone great.
Could bring the steam trains back.

I hear again the whistles shrill,
I see the gleaming brass,
And hear the hissing jets of steam,
As 'Kings' and 'Castles' pass.

Great clouds of smoke envelop me
As on the bridge I stand,
They glide and drift like awesome crests,
Across the nearby land.

I glimpse the open firebox and
The orange glow inside;
And the driver with his fireman
Working with skill and pride.

The air is acrid to the taste,
Black smuts fly ev'rywhere.
But honestly there's nothing now,
That with steam can compare.

They were seldom late or faulty
And, if one chanced to be,
There was always a known reason.
For a freak deformity!

Sometimes I stand on Remps Eye Bridge,
Heedless of cold or rain,
Waiting to see and hear and smell,
A steam-engine again.

And as it passes, history
Is borne along the track,
My very being fills with pride,
As memories flood back.

The River Rhondda

Dylan T Jones

The River Rhondda oozes life
not just fish or plankton rife,
but Wrens and Wagtails and
Blackbirds too and Mallard
Duck and Doves that coo.,

And if you glance the sky up
high you'll see king Heron
gliding by, with bill ahead and
legs stretched rear on route to
ocean, lake or weir,.

Red Kite on mountain-side flies
by and Sparrowhawk 'Still', in the
air.,
An optical illusion say? No.
Nature coming home once more.

Mind's Eye

John W Kempton

The mind's eye is a window to the last;
An image seen through our reversed glass.
Back, back to childhood once again,
To a sunlit world. An echoing refrain.

Calling us to landscapes of the past.
Those times one's spirit stands in grass
Of paddocks, where infant feet ran fast.
Time's distance cannot really break this chain;
The mind's eye is the window.

This winding riverbank I see on which we basked,
Its boldered riverbed; the watery stones which masked
Those tiny rainbowed fish which often deigned,
To swim into our bottling jarred domain.
About that secret land no one has asked.
The mind's eye is the window.

A Tribute To Home

Joan Wakeling

Throughout this busy life of mine
I've been to many places;
Met up with old acquaintances;
Been dazzled by new faces.

A luxury cruise on 'Canberra';
A flight to sunny Spain;
The casino at Monte Carlo;
Returning home again.

Soft Italian music;
French cuisine and wine;
A garden in Granada;
Majorca's temperate clime.

So many lovely places;
So much to do and see;
Experiences remembered
By folk like you and me.

But in my heart, a tiny spot
Outshines those other places;
It's filled with special memories
Of loved ones and dear faces.

It's oh, so very special
And, I say this without blushing,
I'll always love it best of all -
It's home; it's here; it's Flushing!

'Flushing is a tiny Cornish fishing village
situated at the mouth of the Penryn River;
it is listed in the guide books as the
warmest spot in the British Isles'.

The Lights Of Home

M Chester

When the moon is high and the
stars are aglow
away up on the fell I love to go
for there enchantment embraces me
as I wander in my reverie.

From the fell I can see a most
beautiful sight
that fills my heart with sheer delight
far below, glistening street lamps
from the town that's my home
beckon to me never more to roam.

Alas my return to stay may never be
and always my heart grieves
silently
but in my dreams I'll wander the fell
and look down on the lights I know
so well.

Dunvegan

Peter C Maxwell

Skirl, birl, twirl,
Skirl, skirl, skirl,
Skirl, birl, twirl,

Play a lament,
For lives that are spent,
In the service of others,
Fathers, mothers, sisters, brothers.
Play a lament.

Skirl, birl, twirl,
Skirl, skirl, skirl,
Skirl, birl, twirl,

Play a lament for Dunvegan,
May the work she began,
Live in the heart of man,
Play a lament for Dunvegan.

Skirl, birl, twirl,
Skirl, skirl, skirl,
Skirl, birl, twirl,

Play, gold medal pipers play,
Play, play, play,
Play all day.

Play till the stars sigh.
Play till the moon cries,
Play, play, play,
Play all day.

Skirl, birl, twirl,
Skirl, skirl, skirl,
Skirl, birl, twirl,

Play a lament,
For lives that are spent
In the service of others,
Fathers, mothers, sisters, brothers.
Play a lament.

Skirl, birl, twirl,
Skirl, skirl, skirl,
Skirl, birl, twirl.

Wight Gem

Edna M Kennett

This rough hewn diamond set in a silver sea,
Cut from the rim of England's southern coast,
The view I see as I approach your shores
Has strange attractions only you can boast.

What is this magic that you hold for me?
What is it draws me back again to you?
Your sandy bays beneath your chalk-white cliffs,
Gardens ablaze with flowers of every hue.

Has time stood still? I think not. For I see
Above thatched cottages with roses dressed,
Old castle ruins sombre in their death,
With modern man disturbing history's rest.

But as you cross this little island Gem,
O'er grassy downlands, hiding in their folds
Small hamlets, village schools and farms
Garlanded with corn fields burnished gold

Remember those who trod this way before.
And on these hills where poet's feet have trod,
Just think on Him who make this isle so fair;
For all this wondrous beauty is of God.

Destiny Of Spring

Anne Trinder

Look at the sky so clear and so bright
Look at the birds in full flight
Softly the breeze is gently blowing
So sure a sign that winter is going.

The trees are beginning to come alive
The plants and the shrubs have all survived
Crocus and snowdrop peep through the soil
Colouring the hedgerows. Oh so loyal.

Even the sea looks so calm and inviting
Watching the seagulls can be so exciting
See the tide slowly covering the land
Leaving its mark foaming in the sand

Now to the people who hurry all day
Rushing and working to earn their pay
Smiling and happy knowing spring is here
Soon it will be summer. Let's all cheer!

But Me - I Love London

J Silver

I've travelled the world from Pole to Pole
I've also been round the Equator
Have heard all the songs that are written about
The great cities, but I know one greater,

They can sing of L A, in the U S of A
But me - I love London
And in France, Gay Paree may be Oooh la la, oui,
But me - I love London
The beauty of Prague and the Southern Camargue
May be worthy of renown
You can keep all those places
Because I hold the aces
My wonderful London Town.

We're catching up fast on the skyscraper scene
In graffiti we're forging ahead
But didn't the great Dr Johnson once say
If you don't like London you're dead?

They can sing of L A, in the U S of A
But me - I love London
And in France, Gay Paree may be Oooh la la, oui,
But me - I love London
You can to New York or the city of Cork
Go to Uppsala or County Down
But the one with the zest
That makes it the best
Is my quite unforgettable, leaving's regrettable
Wonderful London Town
It's the old River Fleet and it's Carnaby Street
It's a clean subway train and it's Petticoat Lane
It's the churches by Wren and the sound of Big Ben
It is all these and more, that is why I adore
My wonderful London Town.

How Green Is The Valley?

Paul Wadge

Giant earth movers travel slowly,
leaving swathes upon the earth,
scaring there for all to see,
open wounds or open cast?

Mining coal to fill the air,
with dust and muck to clog the lungs,
listen, just listen to the earth,
hear her tears and sobs of pain.

Trees, plants and lush green grass,
all are victims of this blight,
cavernous holes soon blot the land,
leaving tales of woe behind.

Green and beautiful was our land,
this before the coal was found,
now replace the green with black,
and mourn the loss of nature's joy.

And when no coal is left to mine,
the moneymen just move on out,
then one more valley they will find,
an end to beauty, clean and bright.

The inspiration of the beauty,
no longer there to see,
just ever growing scars and tears,
and toxin levels rising.

Sea King

Denis Taylor

Let me stand at a yacht's wheel
with the sun warm on my back,
let me look over a pitching stern
and watch the foaming track
of tumbling, churned white water,
like vapour trails in the sky,
where others travel on gleaming wings
at a faster speed than I.

Let me stand at a yacht's wheel
looking far as the eye can see,
on a vast expanse of blue and white
where wind-borne birds fly free;
and wild sea-horses charge in line
to remind me once again
of my constant dream to roam the sea
as the winds and tides ordain.

Let me stand at a yacht's wheel
and feel spindrift sting my face;
to have the words I try to speak
vanish soundlessly in space.
When all I hear is the crash of waves
and the creak of a wind-lashed mast,
as I sway with the wildly plunging bows
in a sea that is running fast.

Let me stand at a yacht's wheel
and taste salt upon my lips,
while the wind that roams the ocean
embraces me and whips
to greater heights the wave caps
of the restless, boundless sea,
as I exult and make believe
that the ocean's king is me!

The Passing Of Winter

F A Rowley

I hear the snow-wind blowing through the gaunt and leafless trees;
It sighs so very softly in the over-hanging eaves,
I walk into the garden but there is little there to please
As I look for life returning to the land.

The sky is dull and leaden. The distant views unclear,
No colour lights the landscape, just misty greys so drear.
The chill air nips my cheeks, my eye sheds forth a tear
As I look for life returning to the land.

But bending low what do I see before my moistened eyes,
Small green shoots are pushing up, crocus! I realise
From the cold damp soil wherein they need no longer hide
And I see life is returning to the land.

These are the heralds of the spring and bright clear days of May.
Of sunny June and all too soon the summer holidays.
So natures great grand cycle rolls slowly on its way
And life again returns throughout the land.

Transformation

Diana Griffiths

In a dither, sipping bitter
Wishing I could be much fitter;
Nonchalantly I would swig.
I was known as 'Mrs Big'
Getting bigger, lacking vigour,
I could hear my colleagues snigger;
All my food was fattening
And my figure thickening;
Always scoffing like a piglet
Cakes and ale and even brisket.

I was plainly like a ferry
Boat a-sailing on the Mersey;
Bulging like a dromedary
In each dress or knitted jersey;
As my wardrobe faced defunction
I began to feel emotion,
In the middle of my luncheon
Guilt washed o'er me like an ocean.

Vowed I'd try to be much thinner
Watch my weight and be a winner.
I determined to survive
Cut the calories and walk not drive;
I would forthwith be more wise
Raise my sights, reduce my size.
Stop my colleagues' cruel jeers,
They would change their tune to cheers!

Now I'm trimmer, much, much slimmer,
In my evening dress I shimmer;
I'm so light I could take wing
In my step there is new spring!
Now I'm dainty as a peri
Happy to be gaily prancing.

Much less wine and beer and sherry.
In my mirror I keep glancing.

No more nibbling on the Q T.
Because I like the new slim me!

Kynance Cove

Frances Coast

Wild horses ride upon each wave
That heads towards the shore

Then, dashed upon the granite rocks
Are lost - forever more.

As each wave strikes a rugged rock
And covers it with spray.

Becomes a waterfall - and
Trickles back towards the bay.

Hard to believe the wildness and
The wonder of it all.

Yet, once seen, it is remembered and
Ne'er lost beyond recall.

It thunders through the 'Blowing-Hole'
The spume flies high above.

And where is all this beauty? - why,
This is Kynance Cove!

Cambridge

Maureen Turner

Shiny black railings along a tree-lined street
Hundreds of bikes to save the students feet!
Glimpse through an arch of a green velvet square
Dewy-coated in the damp morning air.
Flower-boxed windows and old oak doors
Heavy with knowledge above worn stone floors.
Centuries of students have tread the ancient stair,
Rooms of tutors with a fireside chair.
The river flows gently on through time
Through parties and punts and church-bell chime.
Busy streets, shops old and new
Cafes and pubs and street-buskers, too.
Summer visitors wander with camera in hand,
Ask questions in groups or on street-corners stand.
Find the tree famed for Newton's apple,
Admire the splendour of King's College Chapel.
This is the Cambridge I always see
And this is the place where I like to be!

Memorial

John Knight

We met on the train, then in civvy suits,
Soon to be in Khaki, and army boots.
Given a number, not called MP,
Enquired of each other, if we had a sister.
Joined the same platoon, 1940, month of June,
Marched and drilled, drilled and marched,
Frozen in winter, summer parched.

Then came the day, of embarkation,
But, to spoil our elation.
We both went different ways, myself to Gib, Bob to the middle east

We were disappointed, to say the least
Came, after many days, a letter from Egypt to Gibraltar
The wartime post, one could not falter.
Letters went, to and fro, spoke of spirits, high and low
One day, came a letter, marked 'Certified deceased'
' Return to sender'
As I looked at the letter, I knew, unread,
I thought of Bob, in the desert 'dead'

Memories of a tall strong guy, full of life, and merry wit,
Always the same, fighting fit.

It is men like him, made 'Britain Great'
Bob, my friend, my pal, my mate.

To Bob Snook 9th Batt Somerset Light Infantry, Training Batt
Written 1942 , then 31 years old

Peace At Last

Angela Fay Gibson

A quiet and peaceful meadow
Far away from the maddening crowd
My father's final resting place
A wonderful man of whom we were so proud.

The warmth of the sun embracing him
The patter of the rain from the skies above
The whispering wind billowing through the trees
Where he's sheltered in God's haven with love.

He's surrounded by other companions
Some old, but some so young
Snatched away from their loved ones
Before their lives have even begun.

The wild flowers we planted around him
Corn cockles, colchicum and primroses too
Give all his visitors great pleasure
As they pay their respects anew.

My contentment as I walk through this meadow
Which awaits more souls to depart
Is to thank God for the tremendous pleasure
My father gave, with all his heart.

Sandford Mill Weir

David Belson

We used to take picnics to Sandford Mill weir.
We'd spread Mum's best table-cloth over the grass;
Have squashed corrugated tomato-moist sandwiches,
With wasp-bejewelled lard-cake and mugs of stewed tea.

We'd peer at the clear silken sheen of the river,
Not rushing, just easing its way past the weir,
With water-weeds stretched out straight by its current,
Fat fish and *No Fishing* a rod's length apart.

We'd relish the smell of the empty beer-barrels
Racked high at the ' King's Arms' awaiting the dray.
While jaw-cracking wagon-wheel arrowroot biscuits
Were passed through the door of the kidskeepout bar.

Me and the boys would flip fag-cards and milk-tops
Or ricochet pebbles towards the far bank.
We'd shake up our Smithscrispsandbluetwistofsalt bags
And swig ginger-beer and bottlesofpop.

My head rang with sounds of men's banter and laughter
And chafing that never seemed funny to me
And their shouts as Aunt Sally sticks knocked down the dolly
Or bounced off the iron and the mattress beyond.

Those warm summer evenings brought tied aching legs
And a ride on Dad's neck, 'Just as far as that tree'.
Itchy gnat-bites and bramblebush scratches.
'All gone by morning!' of course, he was right.

Ebb Tide

Jean Silvester

To watch the sea roll over crag and rock
where seagulls poise and cry and mock.
'Tis music oft in mournful dirge
but then again, my emotions surge to this
ever-changing sight.
If time were un-ending, my life would be,
to welcome the dusk, to see the silver
strip that ripples in white-whipped
whirlpools to the shore.
Gone to-day, then I must wait till darkness
gives her beauty back to me.
Could I but tell the freedom and bliss
in this, that others fail to see.

A Walk Through The Woods

R Sandford

The path is strewn with broken twigs
A brook with water clear,
Overhanging willow trees
The sky above so near
Fungus on the bark of trees
Mushrooms white and red
Squirrels scurry on the path
With leaves to make a bed.
A carpet rich with rotting leaves
Scattered all around,
Gigantic roots of trees so tall
Are seen above the ground.
The blackbird calls out to his mate
They flit from tree to bush
The rabbits nibble, dart about
Then down their burrow rush.
The rhododendrons spear shaped leaves
Flower clusters red as wine
The feathered fern grows everywhere
Each tender leaf so fine.
The bright green moss surrounding stones
Encase decaying logs
The black wet mud close by a pool
That is occupied by frogs.
Primroses, violets and bluebells
Are the woodlands most colourful flowers
Take a walk through the woods today
I know you will linger for hours.

America

Barbara Hodder

To USA. I made a visit
And Florida I found exquisite.
In Jacksonville I resided
And on many trips was guided
The people there were very kind.
The avenues were all tree lined.
Houses built for gracious living
In a style for party giving.
Food was great and service cute,
No appetite could fail to suit.
Committees worked for funds to raise,
Churches filled, the Lord to praise.
Cousin dear, you did your share,
To come again will be my prayer.

Home Sweet Home

A Macaskill

Behind closed doors at the end of the day
drapes drawn, lamps on, music in play,
just for a while my plastic smile
can melt into a yawn
and I can be 'myself', 'just me';
no need to put a face on.

Within these walls I pamper and preen,
look at a book, or view the screen;
safe in my niche with my favourite dish
and perhaps a refreshment or two,
away from the loud bustling crowd
and all the hullabaloo.

Sincerely, home is special to me,
a heavenly haven and I have the key;
hearts are mended, wounded pride tended;
problems solved without sorrow.
I've always thought it's better not
to let the sun set on a quarrel.

My home is joyful, a happy place.
It glows, it does, with love always.
On a stormy day, cold and grey,
golden sunbeams glisten and spill
from every rafter, to filter through laughter
while the rest of the world stands still.

Dream Footprints

Christine M Mackenzie

The station, the steam, the train moves away,
The start of our holiday, oh what a day!
Through Paisley and Greenock and on to Wemyss Bay,
Our bikes in the guards van, no extra to pay.

Then out of the carriage, bikes out of the van,
We ride the wood tunnel as fast as we can.
The steamer awaits us with funnel a-smoke,
The crew help us board her with laughter and joke.

The paddles churn round frothing up in the sea,
The engines are pumping the seagulls cry free,
The taste of the salt in the fresh quickening breeze,
We're off to the island of rock, sand and trees.

We meet up with friends from years gone before,
And all of us anxious to be first ashore
We bump up the gangplank, jump into the saddle,
And off to the cafe, the beach or a paddle.

The whole of our holiday stretched out before us,
Two weeks in Millport, oh isn't it glorious!
And now in my sixties it still makes me smile
As I live out my days on this favourite wee Isle.

I walk my own footprints o'er water and sand,
I love every inch of the rocks and the land,
The summers are great, but the winter is too,
To be here all year is for dreams to come true.

Portmahomack

Zoë Gray

A little village by the sea,
Was visited yearly by my siblings and me,
All day long we'd bathe or we'd sail,
Or carry lug-worm around in a pail,
At night we would dress and go to a dance,
Looking for fun or a little romance.
We're all grown up now and drifted away,
But I'll always remember and cherish those days.

The other villages all around,
Were not as quaint as the one we'd found.
There was Rockfield and Balintore,
And another three or four or more.
But now these things have all changed,
Since the oil into Scotland has now ranged.
The local people lost their trust,
In 'foreigners' and the upper crust.

My little village is now quite big,
And those who live there work at Nigg,
And all my childhood friends are wed,
With little kids to put to bed.
I regard it as a poetic place,
But still can't believe its change of face.
With nostalgia I often look back,
For I'll never forget Portmahomack.

The Alcoholic's Plea

Walter Jarvie

Is it nothing to you - all who pass by
That the earth is my mattress, and my blankets the sky
My only one life is severely restricted
To alcohol, I'm really addicted.

Most pass me by, I seem a bother
Yet in God's eyes, I am their brother
Some laugh at me, indeed some do jeer
All because of that first pint of beer.

You'll find me often on poverty's seat
Hoping and praying for something to eat
Even a morsel - to keep hunger away
As I oftimes had nothing, since yesterday.

I call you young folk, and I want you to hear
Please, don't ever take that first pint of beer
For the earth's still my mattress, and God knows on high
That during the harsh winter - my blankets the sky.

For there's folks like me in every land
So please, do try and understand
And tell your heart, when you hear me cry
There, but for the grace of God - go I

A Special Place

Mary Tiffney

High in the hill a rippling rill
receives the melting snow.
Blest is the rain that blends the twain
to swell the stream below.
Where eagles fly and curlews cry
fast flows the tumbling tide
in twist and turn on runs the burn
to meet the ocean wide.
The thirsty earth enjoys rebirth
with benison from the sun.
Great rushing river, lasting life giver
slow down! your task is done.

A breeze through the trees
sets leaves aquiver,
Filtered sun dapples down
on the rippling wave of the river.
Let water flow serene and slow
to make a limpid lake.
Memories start to waken my heart
for old times sake.
On the bark of our trysten-tree
with misted eyes I see
our names engraven.
Troubled and storm tossed
fearful of being lost here was our haven.

I stand alone. My love has gone
to the mistress he loved more than me.
He'll never return. Just like the burn,
he'll always belong to the sea.
Swans gliding, pairing, serenely uncaring;
that I am bereft.
Trout aren't aware. They sleepily stare
from out a rock cleft.

The limpid pool offers me
end of my misery.
Quietus. I'm free.
Blessed life-taker, I go to my maker.
At one with the sun
and the land and the sea.

Catching The Rhythm

Colin Vance

High from the headlights,
Inner city vibe,
Charm and elegance,
Irresistible tribe,
Profound in its way,
A character of intelligence,
Never seen in the shadows,
Never imitated as such,
Full marks to the creator,
The followers with flair,
High quality action,
For those who would dare,
In a provocative way,
The sensual attraction,
A blend of charisma,
Onto this satisfaction,
As were swaying our bodies
To the sounds on the street,
And dancing to another one of those funky beats.

Sanctuary

Mhairi Alexis Maclachlan

At last a shelter safe from harm
No lust no fate no tempting charm
I had envisaged a place bright green
But, here we're clear and can be seen

All my love I give to you
And yes believe me, please, it's true
My arms they'll stay forevermore
We can walk along the shore

A straight blue line, a twinkling star
Forever wondering where you are
Now I see a place bright blue
We're safe here, me and you

A place called love that is our home
Free forever, together to roam
A safety net, a blossom flower
Together we have made the greatest power.

Wild Waterfall

Maria Stuart

A wild waterfall cascades into a rock pool
Invigorating crystal water clear and cool
Golden sunlight radiates the brilliant fall
A vision of beauty to enchant us all

Flowing water reflect golden sunbeams
And iridescent rainbow gleams
Drenching the plants on the ground
The song of the waterfall is a gushing sound

Wild waterfall crystal and cool
Your wild beauty brings peace to the soul
You reflect the panorama of the blue skies
Changing colour to enchant my eyes

The enchanting of the waterfall
Mingles with a sky larks call
Glistening waterfall flowing over a hill
Splashing your crystal beauty in to a rock pool

Beneath An Apple Tree Bough

J Millington

Nature's balm for a fevered brow,
On a summer's eve,
To sit beneath an apple tree bough,
Where peace starts to weave.

To close one's eyes and feel the flow
Of gentleness steal,
Taking the sorrow and aggro,
Helping the heart and mind to heal.

Soothing away the pain of the day.
Relaxing tense muscles,
Like a tender hand, soothing away,
Banishing hustles.

Easing one's eyes of strain to see:
Hear the bees: use time.
Heaven is under the apple tree;
It costs not a dime.

Waiting For You

Lyn Godfrey

In my dreams I see you there
Waiting on the sand
You gaze into the distance
An empty sorry man

I watch you with eyes that cannot see
Out of an empty mind
You gaze into the distance
The sad one left behind

I'm the lucky one I have my place
Happy in the past
You frown into the distance
Life must seem so harsh

In my dreams I wait for you
Longing to touch your face
You smile into the distance
You've found my special place

River Sanctum

Julie Whale

Come awhile and sit with me
In this, my special place.
Relax - don't talk - just listen.
Let the sun shine on your face.
That bridge to your left is very old.
With moss and lichen faded.
Some say a bridge was standing there
When first the land was raided
By warrior Vikings from across the seas.
Who came for spoil and plunder.
Out there in the middle the water is deep.
Look quickly and you will see fish that leap,
Or catch a kingfisher's darting hue
While overhead the skies are blue.
Those piping cries? oh they are the birds
That live on the river marshes
Peopled by gentle cows that graze
And sheep with new-born lambs that laze
Amongst the many wild flowers
That bloom unseen in the daylight hours
While life rushes by beyond those hills, out of sight -
In all the towns and cities.
It makes one sad, fills a heart with pity,
To think such treasure will lie unseen
In the heart of a paradise, totally green.
An undiscovered heaven.
Except to you and me.

Childhood In Glasgow

Helen Johanson

Life on the meanstest was very hard
Lines of washing hung in our back yard
The women stood at the kitchen sink
Rubbing their clothes on boards of zinc

These women so proud kept their wee houses clean
Made nourishing soup from marrow bones so lean
Porridge for breakfast stewed saccharine tea
We drank from jam jars so happily

Their weans were many and pleasures rare
But every night they brushed our hair
With bits of rags they wound our ringlets
Then put us to bed with holes in our singlets

As well as their endless worries and fears
Pawn brokers grew fat on the poor's salty tears
Their Sunday clothes pressed and well brushed
On Monday morn to the pawn they were rushed

We mustn't forget the worst offenders
In a class of their own the money lenders
Half-a-crown each week they charged in the pound
If a payment was missed they charged a crown

They couldn't afford the doctor's high fees
Home-made remedies were used for cut knees
Iodine killed all germs from the mud
Sulphur and treacle purified our blood

Our grannies could cure cuts and sneezes
But couldn't beat those deadly diseases
T B. Scarlet Fever Dipheria too
Pneumonia and Polio to name but a few

Then in the year of forty eight
The poor were rescued from this fate
Free national health the government's plan
Those infectious diseases fled our land

Now it's nineteen ninety and more
Prescription charges just soar and soar
T B is increasing day by day
As hospital beds just fade away

Free national health is on the way out
The meanstest is back without a doubt
The price for the rich increasing their wealth
Is to send us back down that road of ill health

Homeland

H R Cullen

Oh! the beauty of the hills, the mountain tops and valleys steep.
The rocky cliffs and awesome crags with stony slopes and wind-swept paths;
With Cadair looming overhead, snow-capped summit looking down.
A wild, proud land that never bowed its head.

Tho' many came with fierce intent and castles built the land around,
To subjugate the native Prince and fiercely loyal men.
All failed to quell the passionate love, the love of home
That makes this Wales so very rare and Welsh folk what they are.

A love of country, pride of race, with gifts of music and of voice,
To tell the world in every way of fiercest love and joy,
In earth and sky and mountain top, the beauty there
That makes the structure of their race, in every man and boy.

War-Time Memories Abroad

John Chincotta

When I was a child abroad I was sent
To a far-flung land where four years I spent.
At least, to me, it seemed to be
For I had never been to sea.
Nor, for that matter away from home
But in this quest I was not alone.
The second world war would so ensure
That mothers and offspring should endure
Mass evacuation to faraway lands
Lest Gibraltar should fall into hostile hands.
Portuguese neutrality offered a safe haven
So with meagre belongings we were fully laden
To bravely face gigantic waves so steep
And enemy subs, lurking in the deep.
Eventually, the many anxious hours passed
Our 'tourist' destination had been reached at last.
As our brave ship anchored on this final day
Rowing boats raced towards us across the bay
Laden with fine wares most certainly hand-made
Male occupants shouting as they plied their trade.
Some of them were daring youths who, to my surprise,
Dived to retrieve coins and seemed never to arise.
I suffered their fate in waters underneath
But surface they did, coins clenched between their teeth.
Our mothers' thoughts were with the war unkind
And the fate of their men-folk left behind
But for us children there were challenges to come
Unknown terrain, even a new-found love for some.
Unfamiliar words and coins became a must
To city dwellers in rural wanderlust.

Not so long ago I did return
For this yearning never ceased to burn.
I reminisced about, what in adventures learnt
Where as a child evacuee I had been sent.

The sung sad 'fados' which still haunt the mind
Are some memories which still do us bind.
The bullock carts no longer grace the scene
Amid the scented flowers and the green
In this, a veritable paradise
Called Madeira - can one better surmise?

Steve

Gail Weingartner

Through bleak and bad times, always there,
true love, affection, tenderness, care.
My tower of strength, pillar of might,
when all could be seen, was black of night.

Agony, weariness, during my hell, undertaking the role
of reinforcing his iron to enter my soul.
No excuse needed maybe to wander,
the grass tempting greener, there out yonder.

But never to falter, supporter, succourer, forever encouraging,
plunging into his hell and sinking, yet still camouflaging.
A glimpse now at the end of 'our tunnel' . . . a light,
the finish, omega, the harvest of our fight.

Not only my stalwart, nor just lover, more than best friend,
life tarried awhile, but now forward, the future,
together forever until our very end . . .

Benghazi, January '41, '42, '43

Rannoch Melville Russell

Here, in this hard won resting place amid the sand,
Heart of Cyrene's beauteous mistress, second in the land
Of Libya, we rested, stilling the excitement of the chase,
Gazing on the Middle Sea, seeing the second downfall of a race.

Refreshed, inspired to conquest, afield again into the west
We went, pursuers where we had pursued, and blessed
With victory, and prevision of a day fast drawing near
When, westing still, we sight a land grown lately dear.

Thrice we had looked into the west from here across the sea
To our far green land, and twice were made to flee
This place, our honour lost, and naught to show but waste -
Do we no more go easting? is it westing now in haste?

But east or west, whatever fortune turns the war today,
Is graven deep into my heart that city and that laden bay
Where thrice in hope, and twice in blackest fear
We looked into the west and saw our land - so near.

Field Of Dreams

Maureen Gard

Birds on the wing, so high in the air
Break the unblemished blue of the sky
Lying on a bed of soft green grass
Breath escapes in a lingering sigh.

Butterflies flit over grassy tufts
Golden buttercups gleam in the sun,
A tapestry of colour before the eyes
Each flower defending the space it has won.

The magical sound of birdsong
And calming murmur of the bees,
Gossamer threads of a spider
Blowing gently on the breeze.

Joyously carefree a rabbit appears
Hopping, skipping on and on.
Then it stops, ears pricked, sensing danger
In the blink of a eye it is gone.

A solitary tree stands sedately
Unmistakingly the mighty oak
Grandly surveying its kingdom
Branches spread like a windblown cloak.

Morning drifts into afternoon
there surely is no haste,
To leave this tranquil meadow
And join the human rat race.

The soothing sounds of a summers day
Tinkling water from a nearby creek,
The earth beneath warms my body
And the sun caresses my cheek.

Muffled sounds from a distant village
Bring me back from my reverie,
I have to return to the real world
Although here I would much rather be.

It's hard to leave this beautiful place
My heaven on earth it seems,
But tomorrow will bring another day
To bring me back to my field of dreams.

Imaginable Mirage

Janet Johnson

Separated from body lifted towards light
travelling upwards drifting in flight
silent peaceful gliding with grace
past life flashes by in amazing haste

Life's great secret suddenly unfolds
infants hold answers in their souls
innocent bare, bewildered, free from pain
no matter how long life's journey

it ends with the beginning again

A Beautiful Day

Blanche Middleton

The tide was slowly ebbing as we walked on the sand
I turned to you, and stole a kiss, you gently took my hand,
We walked slowly side by side, revelling in our love
The sun was shining brightly, in a azure sky above,
We talked of all the things that we like to do.
Intercepted, by those three words, I love you,
Sitting on the rocks watching waves foaming at their tip
Crashing on the sand, up and down they dipped.
The moon; barely a shadow glinting in the sun.
Waiting for its turn to shine, when daylight is done.
In our darkest hours, when we are far apart.
And we're feeling lonely there's an ache in our heart,
There will be a glint of sunshine towards which we can reach,
By recalling the memory, of our beautiful day on the beach.